Preach the Word

Letters and Sermons from Early Christian Pastors

# PREACH THE WORD

## Letters and Sermons from Early Christian Pastors

Edited by
SILOUAN THOMPSON

PREACH THE WORD

*Letters and Sermons from Early Christian Pastors*



Published by Silouan Thompson
244 Jackrabbit Lane
Kennewick WA 99337
silouanthompson.net

ISBN: 979-8-89778-868-2 (Paperback)
ISBN: 979-8-89778-862-0 (Hardcover)

*Preach the word; be instant in season, out of season; reprove, rebuke, exhort with all long suffering and doctrine.*

*–2 Timothy 4:2*

# Table of Contents


Introduction ........ i

1. Clement of Rome ........ 1
2. The Didache ........ 41
3. Ignatius of Antioch ........ 53
4. Polycarp of Smyrna ........ 95
5. Melito of Sardis ........ 119
6. Athanasius of Alexandria ........ 141

Bibliography ........ 189

Scripture Index ........ 191

# Introduction

## Why this book exists

This book began in a series of readings I undertook over twenty-five years ago. I wanted to demonstrate that the central tenets of my faith – the Trinity, the divinity of Christ, the order of Christian worship – were not merely imposed on the text of scripture, but were shared by every generation of Christians, back to the earliest communities who first received the newly-written letters that became our New Testament. I wanted to be able to say with certainty that I, and the people I was serving as a pastor, were in the mainstream of normal Christian faith and practice.

The early Christians had most of the same biblical texts we have today. How did they read them, teach them, and put them into action? How do our contemporary beliefs and applications of scripture compare to what was being believed and done in the first, second, or third centuries by Christian communities who still had the living memory of the apostles' teaching? It turned out that the Christians of the first few centuries were not silent, and their words were not lost; it was possible to let them speak in their own words.

In the pages that follow, these early Christian writers will address one another – not usually to convince the reader of a new doctrine, but to exhort one another to faithfulness, unity, and service to Christ and his people. What they *assume* will be even more enlightening than what they assert.

My prayer is that the reader will have the opportunity to hold up the faith of the first Christians as a lens through which to evaluate the beliefs and practices of twenty-first century Christianity.

## About the Texts

The sermons and letters presented here are chosen from a wealth of writing by early Christians, including pastoral works, apocalypses, apologetics, and gospels. These texts in particular were chosen because of their universal acceptance as authentic, both among ancient Christians and by academic scholars today, and because of their relevance to our own generation's need for a way of life and worship grounded not in internet arguments, or denominational distinctives, but in firsthand testimony of authentic apostolic faith. These letters and sermons also share in common the characteristic of exhorting and explaining, but not attempting to convince or convert the reader.

The letters of Clement, Ignatius, Polycarp, and the *Didache*, are excerpted and adapted from a translation published in 1953 as *Early Christian Fathers*, edited and translated by Cyril C. Richardson. This text passed into the public domain on January 1, 2010. The translation of Melito's *Peri Pascha* was originally published at "Kerux: A Journal of Biblical Theology." The translator was not credited. The text of Athanasius' *On the Incarnation* and *Answering the Jews* is excerpted from the 1944 English translation *On the Incarnation of the Word*, originally credited as "Translated and edited by A Religious of C.S.M.V." This translation was in fact the work of Sister Penelope Lawson, of the Anglican Community of Saint Mary the Virgin in Wantage, England, and is now in the public domain. It was significantly revised for the present book with much reference to *On the Incarnation (Greek and English)*, translated by Archpriest John Behr, and *On the Incarnation of the*

*Word*, translated by Alexander Walker in *Nicene and Post-Nicene Fathers*. This text comes from a somewhat later period than the rest of the material collected here, but it seems important to include because of the clarity of the author's vision of how the incarnation of Christ accomplishes the salvation of mankind, in a period when neither the Nicene Creed nor any formal dogma of penal substitution had yet been enunciated. The essay *Against the Gentiles*, which usually accompanies *On the Incarnation*, is omitted here as it addresses philosophical controversies less applicable outside the writer's fourth-century context.

For consistency, all citations from the Psalms are numbered according to the Septuagint. Other citations are labeled LXX only when the Septuagint, as quoted by the original author, differs significantly from the modern Masoretic Text.

Most of these texts have been extensively adapted and edited for this edition, with counsel from wiser and better-read scholars. Any errors are purely my own.

1

# Clement of Rome

## Introduction

Outside the New Testament writings, the earliest Christian document we possess is a letter of the church at Rome to the church at Corinth. Very ancient tradition ascribes the letter to a writer named Clement who, according to the earliest episcopal lists, was the third bishop of Rome. The importance of the letter lies in the picture it gives us of early Roman Christianity.

This text's most ancient title, in the Coptic text, is *The Letter of the Romans to the Corinthians*. It is usually referred to as 1 Clement, as there is another letter ascribed to the same author. However the so-called Second Letter of Clement has been considered pseudepigraphical since at least the fourth century: Both Eusebius and Jerome write that there is only one recognized letter of Clement.[1]

The letter indicates that it was written amid the second generation of Christians. The persecution under Nero in AD 64 is already past, the Corinthians are viewed as an "ancient church,"

---

1 Eusebius, *Hist. eccl.* IV. 23:11; Jerome, *De Viris Illustribus*, ch. 15.

and in Rome there are those who from youth to old age have lived irreproachable Christian lives. Yet Peter and Paul, martyred about AD 67, can be described as heroes belonging to "our own generation." And while the apostles have passed away, there still survive some whom they appointed as presbyters. Calamities have again befallen the church – these are distinguished from the persecution under Nero, and are generally understood to refer to Domitian's attacks on Christians. A further indication of the letter's early date is that, aside from a few sayings of the Lord, the writer does not quote any of the Gospels. By the mid-second century we will see 1 Clement quoted very often in the letters of Polycarp of Smyrna.

It was nothing extraordinary for leaders of one church to send a letter of advice and warning to another congregation. The apostolic prerogative exercised by Paul had set a wide precedent which was followed by the author of the seven letters in the Revelation, by Ignatius, by Polycarp, by Dionysius of Corinth,[2] by Serapion,[3] and by many others. Each Christian community seems to have felt a sufficient sense of responsibility for the others so that its leaders could admonish them with solicitude. The local churches did not conceive of themselves as isolated and autonomous units, but were part of the wider Church, and were naturally concerned with what happened in other cities. So this document is not written in the name of an individual, but of a congregation. It is very far from a papal decree, though it was doubtless written by one of the leaders of the Roman church. It makes no claim to personal authority; rather, basing itself on the authority of Scripture, it tries to persuade an errant congregation to return to the right way.

While this letter was written in the name of the church of Rome, there can be little doubt that Clement was the author. The Greek manuscripts attribute it to him, and, as early as AD 170, Dionysius of Corinth ascribes it to him. He speaks of it as the

---

[2] Eusebius, *Hist. eccl.*, IV, ch. 23.

[3] *Ibid.*, V, ch. 19; VI, ch. 12.

letter "which was previously written to us through Clement," and he mentions the fact it was still read publicly in the Corinthian church on Sundays[4].

The earliest episcopal lists, those of Hegesippus (d. AD 180) and Irenaeus (d. AD 202), call Clement the third bishop of Rome. During the first century the role of the ruling bishop was still in development, and at least in Rome, the terms "bishop" and "presbyter" do not yet seem clearly distinguished. But, in any case, Clement is writing as one authorized to address the Corinthian Church on behalf of the Church at Rome.

## The Letter of the Romans to the Corinthians

The church of God, living in exile[5] in Rome, to the church of God, exiled in Corinth – to you who are called and sanctified by God's will through our Lord Jesus Christ. Abundant grace and peace be yours from God Almighty through Jesus Christ.

**1** Dear friends, due to the sudden and successive misfortunes and accidents we have encountered,[6] we have, we admit, been rather long in turning our attention to your quarrels. We refer to the abominable and unholy schism, so alien and foreign to those whom God has chosen, which a few impetuous and headstrong fellows have fanned to such a pitch of insanity that your good name, once so famous and dear to us all, has fallen into the gravest ill repute. Has anyone, indeed, stayed with you without attesting the excellence and firmness of your faith? without admiring your sensible and considerate Christian piety? without broadcasting

---

4 *Ibid*, IV, ch. 23.

5 The Greek word implies a colony of aliens without full civic rights. Christians are strangers and pilgrims on earth, their true fatherland being heaven. *Cf.* 1 Peter 2:11; Philippians 3:20; Hebrews 11:9.

6 The reference is to persecution under Domitian.

your spirit of unbounded hospitality?[7] without praising your perfect and trustworthy knowledge? For you always acted without partiality and walked in God's laws. You obeyed your rulers and gave your elders the proper respect. You disciplined the minds of your young people in moderation and dignity. You instructed your women to do everything with a blameless and pure conscience, and to give their husbands the affection they should. You taught them, too, to abide by the rule of obedience and to run their homes with dignity and thorough discretion.

**2** You were all humble and without any pretensions, obeying orders rather than issuing them, more gladly giving than receiving.[8] Content with Christ's rations and mindful of them, you stored his words carefully up in your hearts and held his sufferings before your eyes.

In consequence, you were all granted a profound and rich peace and an insatiable longing to do good, while the Holy Spirit was abundantly poured out on you all. You were full of holy counsels, and, with zeal for the good and devout confidence, you stretched out your hands[9] to almighty God, beseeching him to have mercy should you involuntarily have fallen into any sin. Day and night you labored for the whole brotherhood, that by your pity and sympathy the sum of his elect might be saved. You were sincere and guileless and bore no grudges. All sedition and schism were an abomination to you. You wept for the faults of your neighbors, while you reckoned their shortcomings as your own. You never regretted all the good you did, being "ready for any good deed."[10] Having an excellent and devout character, you did everything in

---

[7] Hospitality is emphasized several times in the letter. It is a virtue appropriate to churches on the great trade route of the Empire, as Corinth was a natural stop between Rome and the East.

[8] *Cf.* Acts 20:35.

[9] Indicating the ancient posture of prayer, standing upright with the hands lifted up.

[10] Titus 3:1.

His fear. The commands and decrees of the Lord were engraved on the tablets of your heart.[11]

**3** You were granted great popularity and growing numbers, so that the word of Scripture was fulfilled: "My beloved ate and drank and filled out and grew fat and started to kick."[12]

From this there arose rivalry and envy, strife and sedition, persecution and anarchy, war and captivity. And so "the dishonored" rose up "against those who were held in honor," those of no reputation against the notable, the stupid against the wise, "the young against their elders."[13] For this reason righteousness and peace are far from you, since each has abandoned the fear of God and grown purblind in his faith, and ceased to walk by the rules of his precepts or to behave in a way worthy of Christ. Rather does each follow the lusts of his evil heart, by reviving that wicked and unholy rivalry,[14] by which, indeed, "death came into the world."[15]

**4** For Scripture runs thus: "And it happened after some days that Cain brought God a sacrifice from the fruits of the earth, while Abel made his offering from the first-born of the sheep and of their fat. And God looked with favor on Abel and on his gifts; but he did not heed Cain and his sacrifices. And Cain was greatly upset and his face fell. And God said to Cain, 'Why are you so sorrowful, and why has your face fallen? If you have made a correct offering but not divided it correctly, have you not sinned?[16] Be still. He will return to you and you shall rule over him.'[17] And Cain said

---

[11] *Cf.* Prov. 7:3.

[12] Deuteronomy 32:15.

[13] Isaiah 3:5.

[14] A key word in this letter opposing schism. "Rivalry" is used in a very broad sense and in Clement's mind is a primary source of evil. With many examples he traces the persecution of the righteous to the jealous hatred which goodness inspires.

[15] Wisdom 2:24.

[16] The implication is that Cain's gift was rejected because he kept back for himself the best parts.

[17] Genesis 4:7 LXX

to his brother Abel, 'Let us go into the field.' And it happened that while they were in the field Cain attacked his brother Abel and killed him."[18]

You see, brothers, rivalry and envy are responsible for fratricide. Because of rivalry our forefather Jacob fled from the presence of his brother Esau. It was rivalry that caused Joseph to be murderously persecuted and reduced to slavery. Rivalry forced Moses to flee from the presence of Pharaoh, the king of Egypt, when he heard his fellow clansman say: "Who made you a ruler or judge over us? Do you want to slay me as you did the Egyptian yesterday?"[19] By reason of rivalry Aaron and Miriam were excluded from the camp. Rivalry cast Dathan and Abiram alive into Hades because they revolted against Moses, God's servant. Because of rivalry David not only incurred the envy of foreigners but was even persecuted by Saul, the king of Israel.

**5** But, passing from examples in antiquity, let us come to the heroes[20] nearest our own times. Let us take the noble examples of our own generation. By reason of rivalry and envy the greatest and most righteous pillars of the Church[21] were persecuted, and battled to the death. Let us set before our eyes the noble apostles: Peter,[22] who by reason of wicked jealousy, not only once or twice but frequently endured suffering and thus, bearing his witness,[23] went to the glorious place which he merited. Out of rivalry and contention, Paul showed how to win the prize for patient endurance. Seven times he was in chains; he was exiled, stoned,

---

18 Gen. 4:3–8 LXX.

19 Exodus 2:14.

20 Literally *athletes, combatants, champions* – borrowing the metaphor from the Greek athletic games. *Cf.* Hebrews 12:1.

21 *Cf.* Galatians 2:9.

22 This praise of Peter and Paul by the bishop of the church at Rome is interesting, though it also occurs in Ignatius (*To the Romans*, ch. 4). This passage is a witness to Peter's martyrdom in Rome under Nero as well as that of Paul.

23 The word "bear witness" is *martureō*, giving us our word for martyrdom (*cf.* Acts 22:20).

became a herald of the gospel in East and West, and won the noble renown which his faith merited. To the whole world he taught righteousness, and reaching the limits of the West, he bore his witness before rulers. And so, released from this world, he was taken up into the holy place and became the greatest example of patient endurance.

**6** To these men who lived such holy lives there was joined a great multitude of the elect who by reason of rivalry were the victims of many outrages and tortures and who became outstanding examples among us. By reason of rivalry women were persecuted in the roles of Danaïds and Dircae.[24] Victims of dreadful and blasphemous outrages, they ran with sureness the course of faith to the finish, and despite their physical weakness won a notable prize. It was rivalry that estranged wives from their husbands and annulled the saying of our father Adam, "This is now bone of my bone and flesh of my flesh."[25] Rivalry and contention have overthrown great cities and uprooted mighty nations.

**7** We are writing in this vein, dear friends, not only to admonish you but also to remind ourselves. For we are in the same arena and involved in the same struggle. Hence we should give up empty and futile concerns, and turn to the glorious and holy rule of our tradition.[26] Let us note what is good, what is pleasing and acceptable to Him who made us. Let us fix our eyes on the blood of Christ and let us realize how precious it is to his Father, since it was poured out for our salvation and brought the grace of repentance to the whole world. Let us go through all the generations and observe that from one generation to another the

---

[24] A reference to spectacles in the arena where criminals were forced to play mythological roles. In legend, Dirce was tied to the horns of a bull and dragged to death. The daughters of Danaïs were married off by being offered as prizes in a foot race. It is likely that Christian girls were thus sexually abused before being martyred.

[25] Genesis 2:23.

[26] Clement's word "tradition" has no technical religious connotation. The word means something handed over and received. Though not always clear in English translations, this is the word used in 1 Corinthians 11:23; 15:3; 2 Thessalonians 2:15; 3:6.

Master "has afforded and opportunity of repentance"[27] to those who are willing to turn to him. Noah preached repentance and those who heeded him were saved. Jonah preached destruction to the Ninevites; and when they had repented of their sins, they propitiated God with their prayers and gained salvation despite the fact they were not God's people.

**8** The ministers of God's grace spoke about repentance through the Holy Spirit, and the Master of the universe himself spoke of repentance with an oath: "For as I live, says the Lord, I do not desire the death of the sinner, but his repentance." He added, too, this generous consideration: "Repent, O house of Israel, of your iniquity. Say to the sons of my people, Should your sins reach from earth to heaven, and be redder than scarlet and blacker than sackcloth, and should you turn to me with your whole heart and say 'Father!' I will heed you as though you were a holy people."[28] And in another place this is what he says: "Wash and become clean: rid your souls of wickedness before my eyes. Cease from your wickedness, learn to behave well, devote yourselves to justice, rescue the wronged, uphold the rights of the orphan and grant the widow justice. And come, let us reason together, says the Lord; and if your sins are like purple, I will make them white as snow, and if they are like scarlet, I will make them white as wool. And if you are willing and heed me, you shall eat the good things of the earth. But if you are unwilling and do not heed me, the sword shall devour you. For it is the mouth of the Lord that has spoken thus."[29] Since, there, he wanted all those he loved to have an opportunity to repent, he confirmed this by his almighty will.

**9** So, then, let us fall in with his magnificent and glorious intention, and let us prostrate ourselves before him as suppliants of his mercy and kindness. Let us turn to his compassion and give up useless ventures and strife, and rivalry that leads to death. Let

---

[27] Wisdom 12:10.

[28] Clement is freely paraphrasing Ezekiel 33:11–27.

[29] Isaiah 1:16–20.

us father our eyes on those who have served his magnificent glory to perfection. Let us take Enoch, for instance, who, because he proved upright by his obedience, was translated and never died. Noah proved faithful in his ministry and preached a new birth to the world. Through him, therefore, the Master saved those living creatures that entered peacefully into the ark.

Abraham, who was called "The Friend," proved faithful in obeying God's words. It was obedience that led him to leave his country, his kindred, and his father's house, so that by leaving a poor country, a lowly kindred, and an insignificant house, he might inherit God's promises. For he told him: "Depart from your country and from your kindred and from the house of your father, and go to a land which I will show you. And I will make you great among the nations and I will bless you and I will make your name great and you will be blessed. And I will bless those who bless you and curse those who curse you, and all the tribes of the earth will be blessed through you."[30] And again, when he separated from Lot, God told him: "Lift up your eyes and from where you now are look to the North, the South, the East, and the West, for all the land that you see I will give you and your seed forever. And I will make your seed like the dust of the earth. If anybody can count the dust of the earth, then your seed will be counted."[31] And again he says: "God led Abraham out and told him: Look up to heaven and count the stars, if you can. That is how numerous your seed will be! And Abraham believed God and this was put down to his credit as an upright deed."[32] Because of his faith and hospitality a son was granted to him in his old age, and he obediently offered him as a sacrifice to God on one of the hills which he indicated. Because of his hospitality and religious devotion, Lot was saved from Sodom, when the whole countryside was condemned to fire and brimstone.

---

[30] Genesis 12:1–3.

[31] Genesis 13:14–16.

[32] Genesis 15:5, 6.

In that way the Master made it clear that he does not forsake those who put their hope on him, but delivers to punishment and torment those who turn away from him. Of this latter, to be sure, Lot's wife became an example. After fleeing the city with him, she changed her mind and fell out with him – with the result that she became a pillar of salt that exists to this day. In this way it was made evident to all that the double-minded and those who question God's power are condemned and become a warning to all generations.

**12** Because of her faith and hospitality Rahab the harlot was saved. For when the spies were sent to Jericho by Joshua the son of Nun, the king of the land learned that they had come to spy on his country. Consequently he sent out men to capture them, intending to arrest them and put them to death. The hospitable Rahab, however, took them in and hid them in a room upstairs under stalks of flax. When the king's men learned of it, they said to her: "The men who are spying on our country went into your house. Bring them out, for this is the king's command." But she at once answered, "The men you seek came into my house, but they immediately departed and are on their way," and she pointed in the opposite direction. And she said to the spies: "I am absolutely certain that the Lord God is handing this country over to you; for fear and terror of you have fallen on all its people. Therefore, when you come to take it, rescue me and my father's house." And they said to her: "It shall be exactly as you say. When you learn of our approach, you shall gather together all your family under your roof and they shall be saved. But whoever is found outside the house will perish." And in addition they gave her a sign that she should hang a piece of scarlet from her house.[33] By this they made it clear that it was by the blood of the Lord that redemption was going to come to all who believe in God and hope on him. You see, dear friends, that not only faith but prophecy as well is exemplified in this woman.

---

[33] Joshua, ch. 2.

**13** Let us then, brothers, be humble and be rid of all pretensions and arrogance and silliness and anger. Let us act as Scripture bids us, for the Holy Spirit says: "Let not the wise man boast of his wisdom or the strong man of his might or the rich man of his wealth. But let him that boasts boast of the Lord; and so he will seek Him out and act justly and uprightly."[34] Especially let us recall the words of the Lord Jesus, which he uttered to teach considerateness and patience. For this is what he said: "Show mercy, that you may be shown mercy. Forgive, that you may be forgiven. As you behave to others, so they will behave to you. As you give, so will you get. As you judge, so you will be judged. As you show kindness, so will you receive kindness. The measure you give will be the measure you get."[35] Let us firmly hold on to this commandment and these injunctions so that in our conduct we may obey his holy words and be humble. For Holy Scripture says, "On whom shall I look except on him who is humble and gentle and who trembles at my words?"[36]

**14** It is right, then, and holy, brothers, that we should obey God rather than follow those arrogant and disorderly fellows who take the lead in stirring up loathsome rivalry. For we shall incur no ordinary harm, but rather great danger, if we recklessly give ourselves over to the designs of men who launch out into strife and sedition to alienate us from what is right. Let us be kind to one another in line with the compassion and tenderness of him who created us. For it is written: "The kind shall inhabit the land, and the innocent shall be left upon it. But those who transgress shall be cut off from it."[37] And again he says: "I saw an ungodly man exalted and elevated like the cedars of Lebanon. But I passed by and, look, he had vanished! And I searched for his place and could

---

[34] *Cf.* Jeremiah 9:23, 24; 1 Samuel 2:10; 1 Cor. 1:31; 2 Cor. 10:17.

[35] *Cf.* Matthew 5:7; 6:14, 15; 7:1, 2, 12; Luke 6:31, 36–38.

[36] Isaiah 66:2.

[37] Proverbs 2:21, 22; Psalm 37:9, 38.

not find it. Maintain innocence and have an eye for uprightness, for a man of peace will have descendants."[38]

**15** Let us, then, attach ourselves to those who are religiously devoted to peace, and not to those who wish for it hypocritically. For somewhere it is said, "This people honors me with its lips, but its heart is far removed from me."[39] And again, "They blessed with their mouth, but they cursed with their heart."[40] And again it says: "They loved him with their mouth, but they lied to him with their tongue. Their heart was not straightforward with him, and they were not faithful to his covenant. Therefore let the deceitful lips that speak evil against the righteous be struck dumb."[41] And again: "May the Lord destroy all deceitful lips and the tongue that boasts unduly and those who say, 'We will boast of our tongues; our lips are our own; who is Lord over us?' Because of the wretchedness of the poor and the groans of the needy I will now arise, says the Lord. I will place him in safety: I will act boldly in his cause."[42]

**16** It is to the humble that Christ belongs, not to those who exalt themselves above his flock. The scepter of God's majesty, the Lord Jesus Christ, did not come with the pomp of pride or arrogance, though he could have done so. But he came in humility just as the Holy Spirit said of him. For Scripture reads: "Lord, who has believed what we heard? And to whom has the arm of the Lord been revealed? Before him we announced that he was like a child, like a root in thirsty ground. He has no comeliness or glory. We saw him, and he had neither comeliness nor beauty. But his appearance was ignominious, deficient when compared to man's stature. He was a man marred by stripes and toil, and experienced in enduring weakness. Because his face was turned away, he was dishonored and disregarded. He it is who bears our sins and suffers

---

[38] Psalm 36:35–37.

[39] Isaiah 29:13; Mark 7:6.

[40] Psalm 78:36, 37; 62:4.

[41] Psalm 30:19.

[42] Psalm 11:4–6.

pain for us. And we regarded him as subject to toil and stripes and affliction. But it was for our sins that he was wounded and for our transgressions that he suffered. To bring us peace he was punished: by his stripes we were healed. Like sheep we have all gone astray: each one went astray in his own way. And the Lord delivered him up for our sins; and he does not open his mouth because he is abused. Like a sheep he is led off to be slaughtered; and just as a lamb before its shearers is dumb, so he does not open his mouth. In his humiliation his condemnation ended. Who shall tell about his posterity? For his life was taken away from the earth. Because of the transgressions of my people he came to his death. And I will give the wicked as an offering for his burial and the rich for his death. For he did no iniquity and no deceit was found in his mouth. And the Lord's will is to cleanse him of his stripes. If you make an offering for sin, your soul will see a long-lived posterity. And the Lord's will is to do away with the toil of his soul, to show him light and to form him with understanding, to justify an upright man who serves many well. And he himself will bear their sins. For this reason he shall have many heirs and he shall share the spoils of the strong, because his life was delivered up to death and he was reckoned among transgressors. And he it was who bore the sins of many and was delivered up because of their sins."[43]

And again he himself says: "I am a worm and not a man, a disgrace to mankind and despised by the people. All those who saw me mocked me, they made mouths at me and shook their heads, saying: 'He hoped on the Lord. Let him rescue him, let him save him, since he is pleased with him!'"[44]

You see, dear friends, the kind of example we have been given. And so, if the Lord humbled himself in this way, what should we do who through him have come under the yoke of his grace?

---

[43] Isaiah 53:1–12.

[44] Psalm 21:7–9.

**17** Let us be imitators even of those who wandered around "in the skins of goats and sheep,"[45] and preached the coming of the Christ. We refer to the prophets Elijah and Elisha – yes, and Ezekiel, too – and to the heroes of old as well. Abraham was widely renowned and called the Friend of God. When he gazed on God's glory, he declared in his humility, "I am only dust and ashes."[46] This is what is written about Job: "Job was an upright and innocent man, sincere, devout, and one who avoided all evil."[47] But he was his own accuser when he said, "There is none who is free from stain, not even if his life lasts but a single day."[48] Moses was called "faithful in all God's house"[49] and God used him to bring His judgment on Egypt with scourges and torments. Yet even he, despite the great glory he was given, did not boast; but when he was granted an oracle from the bush, said: "Who am I that you send me? I have a feeble voice and a slow tongue."[50] And again he says, "I am but steam from a pot."[51]

**18** And what shall we say of the famous David? God said of him, "I have discovered a man after my own heart, David the son of Jesse: I have anointed him with eternal mercy."[52] But he too says to God: "Have mercy upon me, O God, according to your great mercy; and according to the wealth of your compassion wipe out my transgression. Wash me thoroughly from my iniquity and cleanse me from my sin, for I acknowledge my transgression and my sin is ever before me. Against you only have I sinned; and I have done evil in your sight. The result is that you are right when you speak and are acquitted when you are judged. For, see, I was conceived in iniquity, and in sin did my mother bear me. For, see,

---

[45] Hebrews 11:37.

[46] Genesis 18:27.

[47] Job 1:1.

[48] Job 14:4, 5.

[49] Numbers 12:7; Hebrews 3:2.

[50] Exodus 3:11; 4:10.

[51] The source of the quote is unknown.

[52] Psalm 88:21; Acts 13:22.

you have loved the truth: you have revealed to me the mysteries and secrets of your wisdom. You shall sprinkle me with hyssop and I shall be cleansed. You shall wash me and I shall be whiter than snow. You will make me hear joy and gladness: the bones which have been humbled shall rejoice. Turn your face from my sins and wipe away all my iniquities. Create in me a pure heart, O God, and renew a right spirit in my very core. Cast me not away from your presence, and do not take your Holy Spirit away from me. Give me back the gladness of your salvation, and strengthen me with your guiding spirit. I will teach your ways to the wicked, and the godless shall turn back to you. Save me from bloodguiltiness, O God, the God of my salvation. My tongue will rejoice in your righteousness. You will open my mouth, O Lord, and my lips will proclaim your praise. For if you had wanted sacrifice, I would have given it. You will not find pleasure in burnt offerings. The sacrifice for God is a broken spirit: a broken and a humbled heart, O God, you will not despise."[53]

**19** The humility and obedient submissiveness of so many and so famous heroes have improved not only us but our fathers before us, and all who have received His oracles in fear and sincerity. Since, then, we have benefited by many great and glorious deeds, let us run on to the goal of peace, which was handed down to us from the beginning. Let us fix our eyes on the Father and Creator of the universe and cling to his magnificent and excellent gifts of peace and kindness to us. Let us see him in our minds and look with the eyes of our souls on his patient purpose. Let us consider how free he is from anger toward his whole creation.

**20** The heavens move at his direction and peacefully obey him. Day and night observe the course he has appointed them, without getting in each other's way. The sun and the moon and the choirs of stars roll on harmoniously in their appointed courses at his command, and with never a deviation. By his will and without dissension or altering anything he has decreed the earth becomes

---

[53] Psalm 50:1-19.

fruitful at the proper seasons and brings forth abundant food for men and beasts and every living thing upon it. The unsearchable, abysmal depths and the indescribable regions of the underworld are subject to the same decrees. The basin of the boundless sea is by his arrangement constructed to hold the heaped up waters, so that the sea does not flow beyond the barriers surrounding it, but does just as he bids it. For he said, "Thus far you shall come, and your waves shall break within you."[54] The ocean which men cannot pass, and the worlds beyond it, are governed by the same decrees of the Master. The seasons, spring, summer, autumn, and winter, peacefully give way to each other. The winds from their different points perform their service at the proper time and without hindrance. Perennial springs, created for enjoyment and health, never fail to offer their life-giving breasts to men. The tiniest creatures come together in harmony and peace. All these things the great Creator and Master of the universe ordained to exist in peace and harmony. Thus, he showered his benefits on them all, but most abundantly on us who have taken refuge in his compassion through our Lord Jesus Christ, to whom be glory and majesty forever and ever. Amen.

**21** Take care, dear friends, that his many blessings do not turn out to be our condemnation, which will be the case if we fail to live worthily of him, to act in concert, and to do what is good and pleasing to him. For he says somewhere, "The Spirit of the Lord is a lamp which searches the hidden depths of the heart."[55]

Let us realize how near he is, and that none of our thoughts or of the ideas we have escapes his notice. It is right, therefore, that we should not be deserters, disobeying his will. Rather than offend God, let us offend foolish and stupid men who exalt themselves and boast with their pretensions to fine speech. Let us reverence the Lord Jesus Christ whose blood was given for us. Let us respect those who rule over us. Let us honor our elders. Let us rear the

---

[54] Job 38:11.

[55] Proverbs 20:27.

young in the fear of God. Let us direct our women to what is good. Let them show a purity of character we can admire. Let them reveal a genuine sense of modesty. By their reticence let them show that their tongues are considerate. Let them not play favorites in showing affection, but in holiness let them love all equally, who fear God. Let our children have a Christian training. Let them learn the value God sets on humility, what power pure love has with him, how good and excellent it is to fear him, and how this means salvation to everybody who lives in his fear with holiness and a pure conscience. For he is the searcher of thoughts and of desires. It is his breath which is in us; and when he wants to, he will take it away.

**22** Now Christian faith confirms all this. For this is how Christ addresses us through his Holy Spirit: "Come, my children, listen to me. I will teach you the fear of the Lord. What man is there that desires life, and loves to see good days? Keep your tongue from evil and your lips from uttering deceit. Refrain from evil and do good. Seek peace and follow after it. The eyes of the Lord are over the upright and his ears are open to their petitions. But the face of the Lord is turned against those who do evil, to eradicate their memory from the earth. The upright man cried out and the Lord heeded him and delivered him out of all his troubles. Many are the plagues of the sinner, but his mercy will enfold those who hope on the Lord."[56]

**23** The all-merciful and beneficent Father has compassion on those who fear him, and with kindness and love he grants his favors to those who approach him with a sincere heart. For this reason we must not be double-minded, and our souls must not harbor wrong notions about his excellent and glorious gifts. Let that verse of Scripture be remote from us, which says: "Wretched are the double-minded, those who doubt in their soul and say, 'We have heard these things even in our fathers' times, and, see, we have grown old and none of them has happened to us.' You

[56] Psalm 33:12–18; 31:10.

fools! Compare yourselves to a tree. Take a vine: first it sheds its leaves, then comes a bud, then a leaf, then a flower, and after this a sour grape, and finally a ripe bunch."[57] You note that the fruit of the tree reaches its maturity in a short time. So, to be sure, swiftly and suddenly his purpose will be accomplished, just as Scripture, too, testifies: "Quickly he will come and not delay, and the Lord will come suddenly into his temple, even the Holy One whom you expect."[58]

**24** Let us consider, dear friends, how the Master continually points out to us that there will be a future resurrection. Of this he made the Lord Jesus Christ the first fruits by raising him from the dead. Let us take note, dear friends, of the resurrection at the natural seasons. Day and night demonstrate resurrection. Night passes and day comes. Day departs and night returns. Take the crops as examples. How and in what way is the planting done? The sower goes out and casts each of his seeds in the ground.[59] When they fall on the ground they are dry and bare, and they decay. But then the marvelous providence of the Master resurrects them from their decay, and from a single seed many grow and bear fruit.

**25** Let us note the remarkable token which comes from the East, from the neighborhood, that is, of Arabia. There is a bird which is called a phoenix. It is the only one of its kind and lives five hundred years. When the time for its departure and death draws near, it makes a burial nest for itself from frankincense, myrrh, and other spices; and when the time is up, it gets into it and dies. From its decaying flesh a worm is produced, which is nourished by the secretions of the dead creature and grows wings. When it is full-fledged, it takes up the burial nest containing the bones of its predecessor, and manages to carry them all the way from Arabia to the Egyptian city called Heliopolis. And in broad daylight, so that everyone can see, it lights at the altar of the sun and puts

---

[57] The source of this citation is unknown.

[58] Malachi 3:1.

[59] *Cf.* Matthew 13:3ff.

them down there, and so starts home again. The priests then look up their dated records and discover it has come after a lapse of five hundred years.[60] Shall we, then, imagine that it is something great and surprising if the Creator of the universe raises up those who have served him in holiness and in the assurance born of a good faith, when he uses a mere bird to illustrate the greatness of his promise? For he says somewhere: "And you shall raise me up and I shall give you thanks"[61] and, "I lay down and slept: I rose up because you are with me."[62] And again Job says, "And you will make this flesh of mine, which has endured all this, to rise up."[63]

**27** With this hope, then, let us attach ourselves to him who is faithful to his promises and just in his judgments. He who bids us to refrain from lying is all the less likely to lie himself. For nothing is impossible to God save lying.[64] Let us, then, rekindle our faith in him, and bear in mind that nothing is beyond his reach. By his majestic word he established the universe, and by his word he can bring it to an end. "Who shall say to him, What have you done? Or who shall resist his mighty strength?"[65] He will do everything when he wants to and as he wants to. And not one of the things he has decreed will fail. Everything is open to his sight and nothing escapes his will. For "the heavens declare God's glory and the firmament proclaims the work of his hands. Day pours forth words to day; and night imparts knowledge to night. And there are neither words nor speech, and their voices are not heard."[66]

**28** Since, then, he sees and hears everything, we should fear him and rid ourselves of wicked desires that issue in base deeds.

---

60 The story of the phoenix was famous in antiquity. It is found in Hesiod, Herodotus, Ovid, Pliny the Elder, etc.

61 Source unknown. *Cf.* Psalm 27:7.

62 Psalm 3:5.

63 Job 19:26.

64 *Cf.* Hebrews 6:18.

65 Wisdom 12:12.

66 Psalm 18:1–3.

By so doing we shall be sheltered by his mercy from the judgments to come. For where can any of us flee to escape his mighty hand? What world is there to receive anyone who deserts him? For Scripture says somewhere: "Where shall I go and where shall I hide from your presence? If I go up to heaven, you are there. If I go off to the ends of the earth, there is your right hand. If I make my bed in the depths, there is your spirit."[67] Where, then, can anyone go or where can he flee to escape from the one who embraces everything?

**29** Therefore we must approach him with our souls holy, lifting up pure and undefiled hands to him, loving our kind and compassionate Father, who has made us his chosen portion. For thus it is written: "When the Most High divided the nations, when he dispersed the sons of Adam, he fixed the boundaries of the nations to suit the number of God's angels.[68] The Lord's portion is his people, Jacob: Israel is his allotted inheritance."[69] And in another place it says: "Behold, the Lord takes for himself a people from among the nations, just as a man takes the first fruits of his threshing floor; and the Holy of Holies shall come forth from that nation."[70]

**30** Since, then, we are a holy portion, we should do everything that makes for holiness. We should flee from slandering, vile and impure embraces, drunkenness, rioting, filthy lusts, detestable adultery, and disgusting arrogance. "For God," says Scripture, "resists the arrogant, but gives grace to the humble."[71] We should attach ourselves to those to whom God's grace has been given. We should clothe ourselves with concord, being humble, self-controlled, far removed from all gossiping and slandering, and

---

[67] Psalm 138:7, 8.

[68] The idea is that each nation has its guardian angel.

[69] Deuteronomy 32:8, 9.

[70] A conflation of a number of O.T. phrases: Deuteronomy 4:34; 14:2; Numbers 18:27; 2 Chronicles 31:14; Ezekiel 48:12.

[71] Proverbs 3:34; James 4:6; 1 Peter 5:5.

justified by our deeds, not by words. For it says: "He who talks a lot will hear much in reply. Or does the prattler imagine he is right? Blessed is the one his mother bore to be short-lived. Do not indulge in talking overmuch."[72] We should leave God to praise us and not praise ourselves. For God detests self-praisers. Let others applaud our good deeds, as it was with our righteous forefathers. Presumption, audacity, and recklessness are traits of those accursed by God. But considerateness, humility, and modesty are the traits of those whom God has blessed.

**31** Let us, then, cling to his blessing and note what leads to it. Let us unfold the tale of the ancient past. Why was our father Abraham blessed? Was it not because he acted in righteousness and truth, prompted by faith? Isaac, fully realizing what was going to happen, gladly let himself be led to sacrifice. In humility Jacob quit his homeland because of his brother. He went to Laban and became his slave, and to him there were given the twelve scepters of the tribes of Israel.

**32** And if anyone will candidly look into each example, he will realize the magnificence of the gifts God gives. For from Jacob there came all the priests and the Levites who serve at God's altar. From him comes the Lord Jesus so far as his human nature goes. From him there come the kings and rulers and governors of Judah. Nor is the glory of the other tribes derived from him insignificant. For God promised that "your seed shall be as the stars of heaven."[73] So all of them received honor and greatness, not through themselves or their own deeds or the right things they did, but through his will. And we, therefore, who by his will have been called in Jesus Christ, are not justified of ourselves or by our wisdom or insight or religious devotion or the holy deeds we have done from the heart, but by that faith by which almighty God has justified all men from the very beginning. To him be glory forever and ever. Amen.

---

[72] Job 11:2, 3 LXX.

[73] Genesis 15:5; 22:17; 26:4.

**33** What ought we to do, then, brothers? Should we grow slack in doing good[74] and give up love? May the Lord never permit this to happen at any rate to us! Rather should we be energetic in doing every good work with earnestness and eagerness. For the Creator and Master of the universe himself rejoices in his works. Thus by his almighty power he established the heavens and by his inscrutable wisdom he arranged them. He separated the land from the water surrounding it and fixed it upon the sure foundation of his own will. By his decree he brought into existence the living creatures which roam on it; and after creating the sea and the creatures which inhabit it, he fixed its boundaries by his power. Above all, with his holy and pure hands he formed man, his outstanding and greatest achievement, stamped with his own image. For this is what God said: "Let us make man in our own image and likeness. And God made man: male and female he created them."[75] And so, when he had finished all this, he praised it and blessed it and said, "Increase and multiply."[76] We should observe that all the righteous have been adorned with good deeds and the very Lord adorns himself with good deeds and rejoices. Since, then, we have this example, we should unhesitatingly give ourselves to his will, and put all our effort into acting uprightly.

**34** The good laborer accepts the bread he has earned with his head held high; the lazy and negligent workman cannot look his employer in the face. We must, then, be eager to do good; for everything comes from Him. For he warns us: "See, the Lord is coming. He is bringing his reward with him, to pay each one according to his work."[77] He bids us, therefore, to believe on him with all our heart, and not to be slack or negligent in every good deed. He should be the basis of our boasting and assurance. We should be subject to his will. We should note how the whole throng

---

[74] Galatians 6:9

[75] Genesis 1:26, 27.

[76] Genesis 1:28.

[77] A conflation from: Isaiah 40:10; 62:11; Proverbs 24:12; Revelation 22:12.

of his angels stand ready to serve his will. For Scripture says: "Ten thousand times ten thousand stood by him, and thousands of thousands ministered to him and cried out: Holy, holy, holy is the Lord of Hosts: all creation is full of his glory."[78] We too, then, should gather together for worship in concord and mutual trust, and earnestly beseech him as it were with one mouth, that we may share in his great and glorious promises. For he says, "Eye has not seen and ear has not heard and man's heart has not conceived what he has prepared for those who patiently wait for him."[79]

**35** How blessed and amazing are God's gifts, dear friends! Life with immortality, splendor with righteousness, truth with confidence, faith with assurance, self-control with holiness! And all these things are within our comprehension. What, then, is being prepared for those who wait for him? The Creator and Father of eternity, the all-holy, himself knows how great and wonderful it is. We, then, should make every effort to be found in the number of those who are patiently looking for him, so that we may share in the gifts he has promised. And how shall this be, dear friends? If our mind is faithfully fixed on God; if we seek out what pleases and delights him; if we do what is in accord with his pure will, and follow in the way of truth. If we rid ourselves of all wickedness, evil, avarice, contentiousness, malice, fraud, gossip, slander, hatred of God, arrogance, pretension, conceit, and inhospitality. God hates those who act in this way; "and not only those who do these things but those who applaud them."[80] For Scripture says: "But God told the sinner: Why do you speak of my statutes and have my covenant on your lips? You hated discipline and turned your back on my words. If you saw a thief you went along with him, and you threw in your lot with adulterers. Your mouth overflowed with iniquity, and your tongue wove deceit. You sat there slandering your brother and putting a stumbling

---

[78] Daniel 7:10; Isaiah 6:3.

[79] 1 Corinthians 2:9; Isaiah 64:4.

[80] *Cf.* Romans 1:29–32.

block in the way of your mother's son. This you did, and I kept silent. You suspected, you wicked man, that I would be like you. I will reproach you and show you your very self. Ponder, then, these things, you who forget God, lest he seize you like a lion and there be no one to save you. A sacrifice of praise will glorify me, and that is the way by which I will show him God's salvation."[81]

**36** This is the way, dear friends, in which we found our salvation, Jesus Christ, the high priest of our offerings, the protector and helper of our weakness. Through him we fix our gaze on the heights of heaven. In him we see mirrored God's pure and transcendent face. Through him the eyes of our hearts have been opened. Through him our foolish and darkened understanding springs up to the light. Through him the Master has willed that we should taste immortal knowledge. For, "since he reflects God's splendor, he is as superior to the angels as his title is more distinguished than theirs."[82] For thus it is written: "He who makes his angels winds, and his ministers flames of fire."[83] But of his son this is what the Master said: "You are my son: today I have begotten you. Ask me and I will give you the nations for you to inherit, and the ends of the earth for you to keep."[84] And again he says to him: "Sit at my right hand until I make your enemies your footstool."[85] Who are meant by "enemies"? Those who are wicked and resist his will.

**37** In earnest, then, brothers, we must march under his irreproachable orders. Let us note with what discipline, readiness, and obedience those who serve under our generals carry out orders. Not everybody is a general, colonel, captain, sergeant, and so on. But "each in his own order"[86] carries out the orders of the

---

[81] Psalm 49:16–23.

[82] Hebrews 1:3, 4.

[83] Hebrews 1:7; Psalm 103:4.

[84] Hebrews 1:5; Psalm 2:7, 8.

[85] Hebrews 1:13; Psalm 110:1.

[86] 1 Corinthians 15:23.

emperor and of the generals. The great cannot exist without the small; neither can the small exist without the great. All are linked together; and this has an advantage. Take our body, for instance. The head cannot get along without the feet. Nor, similarly, can the feet get along without the head. "The tiniest parts of our body are essential to it,"[87] and are valuable to the total body. Yes, they all act in concord, and are united in a single obedience to preserve the whole body.

**38** Following this out, we must preserve our Christian body too in its entirety. Each must be subject to his neighbor, according to his special gifts. The strong must take care of the weak; the weak must look up to the strong. The rich must provide for the poor; the poor must thank God for giving him someone to meet his needs. The wise man must show his wisdom not in words but in good deeds. The humble must not brag about his humility; but should give others occasion to mention it. He who is celibate must not put on airs. He must recognize that his self-control is a gift from another. We must take to heart, brothers, from what stuff we were created, what kind of creatures we were when we entered the world, from what a dark grave he who fashioned and created us brought us into his world. And we must realize the preparations he so generously made before we were born. Since, then, we owe all this to him, we ought to give him unbounded thanks. To him be glory forever and ever. Amen.

**39** Thoughtless, silly, senseless, and ignorant folk mock and jeer at us, in an effort, so they imagine, to exalt themselves. But what can a mere mortal do? What power has a creature of earth? For it is written: "There was no shape before my eyes, but I heard a breath and a voice. What! Can a mortal be pure before the Lord? Or can a man be blameless for his actions, if he does not believe in His servants and finds something wrong with His angels? Not even heaven is pure in His sight: let alone those who live in houses of clay – of the very same clay of which we ourselves are made.

[87] 1 Corinthians 12:21, 22.

He smites them like a moth; and they do not last from dawn to dusk. They perish, for they cannot help themselves. He breathes on them, and they die for lack of wisdom. Call out and see if anyone will heed you, or if you will see any of the holy angels. For wrath destroys a stupid man, and rivalry is the death of one in error. I have seen the foolish taking root, but suddenly their home is swept away. May their sons be far from safety! May they be mocked at the doors of lesser men, and there will be none to deliver them. For what has been prepared by them, the righteous will eat; and they shall not be delivered from troubles."[88]

**40** Now that this is clear to us and we have peered into the depths of the divine knowledge, we are bound to do in an orderly fashion all that the Master has bidden us to do at the proper times he set. He ordered sacrifices and services to be performed; and required this to be done, not in a careless and disorderly way, but at the times and seasons he fixed. Where he wants them performed, and by whom, he himself fixed by his supreme will, so that everything should be done in a holy way and with his approval, and should be acceptable to his will. Those, therefore, who make their offerings at the time set, win his approval and blessing. For they follow the Master's orders and do no wrong. The high priest is given his particular duties: the priests are assigned their special place, while on the Levites particular tasks are imposed. The layman is bound by the layman's code.

**41** Brothers, each of us in his own order must win God's approval and have a clear conscience. We must not transgress the rules laid down for our ministry, but must perform it reverently. Not everywhere, brothers, are the different sacrifices – the daily ones, the freewill offerings, and those for sins and trespasses – offered, but only in Jerusalem. And even there sacrifices are not made at any place, but only in front of the sanctuary, at the altar, after the high priest and the ministers mentioned have inspected the offering for blemishes. Those, therefore, who act in any way at

---

[88] Job 4:16–18; 15:15.

variance with his will, suffer the penalty of death. You see, brothers, the more knowledge we are given, the greater risks we run.

**42** The apostles received the gospel for us from the Lord Jesus Christ; Jesus, the Christ, was sent from God. Thus Christ is from God and the apostles from Christ. In both instances the orderly procedure depends on God's will. And so the apostles, after receiving their orders and being fully convinced by the resurrection of our Lord Jesus Christ and assured by God's word, went out in the confidence of the Holy Spirit to preach the good news that God's Kingdom was about to come. They preached in country and city, and appointed their first converts, after testing them by the Spirit, to be the bishops and deacons of future believers. Nor was this any novelty, for Scripture had mentioned bishops and deacons long before. For this is what Scripture says somewhere: "I will appoint their bishops in righteousness and their deacons in faith."[89]

**43** And is it any wonder that those Christians whom God had entrusted with such a duty should have appointed the officers mentioned? For the blessed Moses too, "who was a faithful servant in all God's house,"[90] recorded in the sacred books all the orders given to him, and the rest of the prophets followed in his train by testifying with him to his legislation. Now, when rivalry for the priesthood arose and the tribes started quarreling as to which of them should be honored with this glorious privilege, Moses bid the twelve tribal chiefs bring him rods, on each of which was written the name of one of the tribes.[91] These he took and bound, sealing them with the rings of the tribal leaders; and he put them in the tent of testimony on God's table. Then he shut the tent and put seals on the keys just as he had on the rods. And he told them: "Brothers, the tribe whose rod puts forth buds is the one God has chosen for the priesthood and for his ministry." Early the next

---

89 Isaiah 60:17 LXX.

90 Numbers 12:7; Hebrews 3:5.

91 Numbers ch. 17.

morning he called all Israel together, six hundred thousand strong, and showed the seals to the tribal chiefs and opened the tent of testimony and brought out the rods. And it was discovered that Aaron's rod had not only budded, but was actually bearing fruit. What do you think, dear friends? Did not Moses know in advance that this was going to happen? Why certainly. But he acted the way he did in order to forestall anarchy in Israel, and so that the name of the true and only God might be glorified. To Him be the glory forever and ever. Amen.

**44** Now our apostles knew through our Lord Jesus Christ that there would be strife over the title of bishop. It was for this reason and because they had received an accurate knowledge of the future, that they appointed the servants we have mentioned. Furthermore, they later added a provision so that, should these men fall asleep, other approved men should succeed to their ministry[92]. In light of this, we view it as a breach of justice to remove from their ministry those who were appointed either by the apostles or later on and with the whole church's consent, by others of the proper standing, and who for a long time, bearing a good report with all, have ministered to Christ's flock faultlessly, humbly, quietly, and unassumingly. For we shall be guilty of a great sin if we eject from the office of bishop men who have offered the sacrifices with innocence and holiness. Happy indeed are those presbyters who have gone before, and who ended a life of fruitfulness with their task complete. For they need not fear that anyone will remove them from their secure positions. But you, we observe, have removed a number of people, despite their good conduct, from a ministry they have fulfilled with honor and integrity.

**45** Your contention and rivalry, brothers, thus touches matters that bear on our salvation. You have studied Holy Scripture, which contains the truth and is inspired by the Holy Spirit. You realize that there is nothing wrong or misleading written in it.

---

[92] *Cf.* 2 Timothy 2:2.

You will not find that upright people have ever been disowned by holy men. The righteous, to be sure, have been persecuted, but by wicked men. They have been imprisoned, but by the godless. They have been stoned by transgressors, slain by men prompted by abominable and wicked rivalry. Yet in such sufferings they bore up nobly.

What shall we say, brothers? Was Daniel cast into a den of lions by those who revered God? Or were Ananias, Azarias, or Mishael shut up in the fiery furnace by men devoted to the magnificent and glorious worship of the Most High? Not for a moment! Who, then, was it that did such things? Detestable men, thoroughly and completely wicked, whose factiousness drove them to such a pitch of fury that they tormented those who resolutely served God in holiness and innocence. They failed to realize that the Most High is the champion and defender of those who worship his excellent name with a pure conscience. To him be the glory forever and ever. Amen. But those who held out with confidence inherited glory and honor. They were exalted, and God inscribed them in his memory forever and ever. Amen.

**46** Brothers, we must follow such examples. For it is written: "Follow the saints, because those who follow them will become saints."[93] Again, it says in another place: "In the company of the innocent, you will be innocent; in the company of the elect, you will be elect; and in a crooked man's company you will go wrong."[94] Let us, then, follow the innocent and the upright. It is they who are God's elect. Why is it that you harbor strife, bad temper, dissension, schism, and quarreling? Do we not have one God, one Christ, one Spirit of grace which was poured out on us? And is there not one calling in Christ? Why do we rend and tear asunder Christ's members and raise a revolt against our own body? Why do we reach such a pitch of insanity that we are oblivious of the fact we are members of each other? Recall the words of our

---

[93] Source unknown.

[94] Psalm 17:26, 27.

Lord Jesus. For he said: "Woe to that man! It were better for him not to have been born than to be the occasion of one of my chosen ones stumbling. It were better for him to have a millstone around his neck and to be drowned in the sea, than to pervert one of my chosen."[95] Your schism has led many astray; it has made many despair; it has made many doubt; and it has distressed us all. Yet it goes on!

**47** Pick up the letter of the blessed apostle Paul. What was the primary thing he wrote to you, "when he started preaching the Gospel?" To be sure, under the Spirit's guidance, he wrote to you about himself and Cephas and Apollos, because even then you had formed cliques. But at that time factiousness was a less serious sin, since you were partisans of notable apostles and of a man they approved. But think now who they are who have led you astray and degraded your honorable and celebrated love of the brethren. It is disgraceful, exceedingly disgraceful, and unworthy of your Christian upbringing, to have it reported that because of one or two individuals the solid and ancient Corinthian Church is in revolt against its presbyters. This report, moreover, has reached not only us, but those who dissent from us as well.[96] The result is that the Lord's name is being blasphemed because of your foolishness, and you are exposing yourselves to danger.

We must, then, put a speedy end to this. We must prostrate ourselves before the Master, and beseech him with tears to have mercy on us and be reconciled to us and bring us back to our honorable and holy practice of brotherly love. For it is this which is the gate of righteousness, which opens the way to life, as it is written: "Open the gates of righteousness for me, so that I may enter by them and praise the Lord. This is the gate of the Lord; the righteous shall enter by it."[97] While there are many gates open, the gate of righteousness is the Christian gate. Blessed are all those

---

[95] Matthew 26:24; Luke 17:1, 2.

[96] *I.e.*, Jews and pagans.

[97] Psalm 117:19, 20.

who enter by it and direct their way in holiness and righteousness, by doing everything without disorder.

Let a man be faithful, let him be capable of uttering knowledge, let him be wise in judging arguments, let him be pure in conduct. But the greater he appears to be, the more humble he ought to be, and the more ready to seek the common good in preference to his own.

**49** Whoever has Christian love must keep Christ's commandments. Who can describe the bond of God's love? Who is capable of expressing its great beauty? The heights to which love leads are beyond description. Love unites us to God. "Love hides a multitude of sins."[98] Love puts up with everything and is always patient. There is nothing vulgar about love, nothing arrogant. Love knows nothing of schism or revolt. Love does everything in harmony. By love all God's elect were made perfect. Without love nothing can please God. By love the Master accepted us. Because of the love he had for us, and in accordance with God's will, Jesus Christ our Lord gave his blood for us, his flesh for our flesh, and his life for ours.

**50** You see, brothers, how great and amazing love is, and how its perfection is beyond description. Who is able to possess it save those to whom God has given the privilege? Let us, then, beg and implore him mercifully to grant us love without human bias and to make us irreproachable. All the generations from Adam to our day have passed away, but those who, by the grace of God, have been made perfect in love have a place among the saints, who will appear when Christ's Kingdom comes. For it is written: "Go into your inner chamber for a very little while, until my wrath and anger pass, and I will remember a good day and I will raise you up from your graves."[99] Happy are we, dear friends, if we keep God's commandments in the harmony of love, so that by love our sins may be forgiven us. For it is written: "Happy are those whose

---

[98] Proverbs 10:12; 1 Peter 4:8.

[99] Isaiah 26:20; Ezekiel 37:12

iniquities are forgiven and whose sins are covered. Happy is the man whose sin the Lord will not reckon, and on whose lips there is no deceit."[100] This is the blessing which was given to those whom God chose through Jesus Christ our Lord. To him be the glory forever and ever. Amen.

**51** Let us, then, ask pardon for our failings and for whatever we have done through the prompting of the adversary. And those who are the ringleaders of the revolt and dissension ought to reflect upon the common nature of our hope. Those, certainly, who live in fear and love would rather suffer outrages themselves than have their neighbors do so. They prefer to endure condemnation themselves rather than bring in reproach our tradition of noble and righteous harmony. It is better for a man to confess his sins than to harden his heart in the way those rebels against God's servant Moses hardened theirs. The verdict against them was made very plain. For "they went down to Hades alive,"[101] and "death will be their shepherd."[102] Pharaoh and his host and all the princes of Egypt and the chariots and their riders" were engulfed in the Red Sea and perished, for no other reason than that they hardened their foolish hearts after Moses, God's servant, had done signs and wonders in Egypt.

**52** Brothers, the Master has no need of anything. He wants nothing from anybody save that he should praise him. For his favorite, David, says: "I will praise the Lord; and this will please him more than a young calf with horns and hoofs. Let the poor observe this and rejoice."[103] And again he says: "Offer to God the sacrifice of praise, and pay your vows to the Most High. Call on me in the day of your affliction and I will rescue you, and you will glorify me. For the sacrifice God wants is a broken spirit."[104]

---

[100] Psalm 31:1, 2; Romans 4:7–9.

[101] Numbers 16:33.

[102] Psalm 48:15.

[103] Psalm 68:31–32.

[104] Psalm 49:14, 15; 50:19.

**53** You know well the Holy Scriptures, dear friends, and you have studied the oracles of God.[105] It is to remind you of them that we write the way we do. When Moses ascended the mountain and spent forty days and forty nights in fasting and humiliation, God said to him: "Get quickly down from here, for your people, whom you led out of the land of Egypt, have broken the law. They have quickly turned from the way you bid them take. They have cast idols for themselves."[106] And the Lord told him: "I have spoken to you once, yes, twice, saying, I have looked at this people and, see, it is obstinate. Let me exterminate them, and I will wipe out their name from under heaven, and I will make you into a great and wonderful nation, much larger than this one."[107] And Moses answered: "No, no, Lord. Pardon my people's sin, or else eliminate me too from the roll of the living."[108]

O great love! O unsurpassed perfection! The servant speaks openly to his Lord. He begs pardon for his people or requests that he too will be wiped out along with them.

**54** Well, then, who of your number is noble, large-hearted, and full of love? Let him say: "If it is my fault that revolt, strife, and schism have arisen, I will leave, I will go away wherever you wish, and do what the congregation orders. Only let Christ's flock live in peace with their appointed presbyters." The man who does this will win for himself great glory in Christ; and will be welcome everywhere. "For the earth and its fullness belong to the Lord."[109] This has been the conduct and will always be the conduct of those who have no regrets that they belong to the city of God.

---

[105] 1 Peter 4:11.

[106] Exodus 32:7, 8; Deuteronomy 9:12

[107] Exodus 32:9, 10; Deuteronomy 9:13, 14.

[108] Exodus 32:31, 32.

[109] Psalm 23:1.

**55** Let us take some heathen examples:[110] In times of plague many kings and rulers, prompted by oracles, have given themselves up to death in order to rescue their subjects by their own blood.[111] Many have quit their own cities to put an end to sedition.[112] We know many of our own number who have had themselves imprisoned in order to ransom others. Many have sold themselves into slavery and given the price to feed others. Many women, empowered by God's grace, have performed deeds worthy of men. The blessed Judith, when her city was under siege, begged of the elders to be permitted to leave it for the enemy's camp. So she exposed herself to danger and for love of her country and of her besieged people, she departed. And the Lord delivered Holofernes into the hands of a woman. To no less danger did Esther, that woman of perfect faith, expose herself in order to rescue the twelve tribes of Israel when they were on the point of being destroyed. For by her fasting and humiliation she implored the all-seeing Master, the eternal God; and he beheld the humility of her soul and rescued her people for whose sake she had faced danger.

**56** So we too must intercede for any who have fallen into sin, that considerateness and humility may be granted to them and that they may submit, not to us, but to God's will. For in that way they will prove fruitful and perfect when God and the saints remember them with mercy. We must accept correction, dear friends. No one should resent it. Warnings we give each other are good and thoroughly beneficial. For they bind us to God's will. This is what the Holy Word says about it: "The Lord has disciplined me severely and has not given me up to death. For the Lord disciplines the one he loves, and punishes every son he accepts."[113] For, it says, "the upright man will discipline me with mercy and reprove me. But let not the oil of sinners anoint my

---

[110] The influence of Roman culture on Clement is evident here, as in his references to the phoenix (ch. 25) and to the Roman army (ch. 37).

[111] *Cf.* Cicero, *Tusc.* 1: 116.

[112] *E.g.*, Solon, Lycurgus, Scipio Africanus.

[113] Psalm 117:18; Proverbs 3:12; Hebrews 12:6.

head."[114] And again it says: "Happy is the man the Lord reproves. Do not refuse the Almighty's warning. For he inflicts pain, and then makes all well again. He smites, but his hands heal. Six times will he rescue you from trouble; and on the seventh evil will not touch you. In famine he will rescue you from death; in war he will deliver you from the edge of the sword. From the scourge of the tongue he will hide you, and you will not be afraid of evils when they come. You will ridicule the wicked and lawless, and not be afraid of wild beasts; for wild beasts will leave you in peace. Then you will discover that your house will be peaceful, and the tent in which you dwell will be safe. You will find, too, that your seed will be numerous, and your children like the grass of the fields. You will come to your tomb like ripe wheat harvested at the appropriate season, or like a heap on the threshing floor gathered together at the right time."[115]

You see, dear friends, how well protected they are whom the Master disciplines. Yes, he is like a good Father, and disciplines us so that the outcome of his holy discipline may mean mercy for us. And that is why you who are responsible for the revolt must submit to the presbyters. You must humble your hearts and be disciplined so that you repent. You must learn obedience, and be done with your proud boasting and curb your arrogant tongues. For it is better for you to have an insignificant yet creditable place in Christ's flock than to appear eminent and be excluded from Christ's hope. For this is what the excellent Wisdom says: "See, I will declare to you the utterance of my Spirit: I will teach you my word. Since I called and you did not listen, since I poured out words and you did not heed, but disregarded my plans and disobeyed my reproofs, therefore I will laugh at your destruction. And I will rejoice when ruin befalls you and when confusion suddenly overtakes you, and catastrophe descends like a hurricane, or when persecution and siege come upon you. Yes, it will be like

---

[114] Psalm 141:5.

[115] Job 5:17–26.

this: when you call upon me, I will not heed you. The wicked shall look for me and shall not find me. For they detested wisdom, and did not choose the fear of the Lord. They had no desire to heed my counsels, and mocked at my reproofs. For this reason they shall eat the fruit of their ways and fill themselves with impiety. Because they wronged babes, they will be slain; and by being searched out the impious shall be destroyed. But he that listens to me will dwell in confident hope and live quietly, free from the fear of any misfortune."[116]

**58** So, then, let us obey his most holy and glorious name and escape the threats which Wisdom has predicted against the disobedient. In that way we shall live in peace, having our confidence in his most holy and majestic name. Accept our advice, and you will never regret it. For as God lives, and as the Lord Jesus Christ lives and the Holy Spirit – on whom the elect believe and hope – the man who with humility and eager considerateness and with no regrets does what God has decreed and ordered will be enlisted and enrolled in the ranks of those who are saved through Jesus Christ. Through him be the glory to God forever and ever. Amen.

**59** If, on the other hand, there be some who fail to obey what God has told them through us, they must realize that they will enmesh themselves in sin and in no insignificant danger. We, for our part, will not be responsible for such a sin. But we will beg with earnest prayer and supplication that the Creator of the universe will keep intact the precise number of his elect in the whole world, through his beloved Child[117] Jesus Christ. It was through him that he called us "from darkness to light,"[118] from

---

[116] Proverbs 1:23–33.

[117] *Cf.* Acts 4:27. Greek *paîs* has both the meanings *child* and *servant;* it is applied to Christ in light of the Servant passages of Isaiah (42:1–9, 49:1–7, 50:4–9, and 52:13–53:12) and occurs in early liturgical language.

[118] Acts 26:18.

ignorance to the recognition of his glorious name,[119] to hope on Your name, which is the origin of all creation. You have opened "the eyes of our hearts"[120] so that we realize you alone are "highest among the highest, and ever remain holy among the holy."[121] "You humble the pride of the arrogant, overrule the plans of the nations, raise up the humble and humble the haughty. You make rich and make poor; you slay and bring to life; you alone are the guardian of spirits and the God of all flesh."[122] You see into the depths: you look upon men's deeds; you aid those in danger and "save those in despair."[123]

You are the Creator of every spirit and watch over them. You multiply the nations on the earth, and from out of them all you have chosen those who love you through Jesus Christ, your beloved Son. Through him you have trained us, made us saints, and honored us.

We ask you, Master, be our helper and defender. Rescue those of our number in distress; raise up the fallen; assist the needy; heal the sick; turn back those of your people who stray; feed the hungry; release our captives; revive the weak; encourage those who lose heart. "Let all the nations know that you alone are God,"[124] that Jesus Christ is your Child, and "that we are your people and the sheep of your pasture."[125]

**60** You brought into being the everlasting structure of the world by what you did. You, Lord, made the earth. You who are faithful in all generations, righteous in judgment, marvelous in

---

[119] It is possible that there is a gap in the text at this point. But it may be that the awkwardness of construction is due to the fact that Clement is citing a familiar form of prayer, into which his train of thought has led him.

[120] Ephesians 1:18.

[121] Ephesians 1:18.

[122] A conflation of Biblical phrases. See Isaiah 13:11; Job 5:11; 1 Samuel 2:7 (*cf.* Luke 1:53); Deuteronomy 32:39; 1 Samuel 2:6; 2 Kings 5:7; Numbers 27:16.

[123] Judith 9:11.

[124] 1 Kings 8:60; 2 Kings 19:19; Ezekiel 36:23.

[125] Psalm 78:13; 94:7; 99:3.

strength and majesty, wise in creating, prudent in making creation endure, visibly good, kind to those who trust in you, merciful and compassionate – forgive us our sins, wickedness, trespasses, and failings. Do not take account of every sin of your slaves and slave girls, but cleanse us with the cleansing of your truth, and "guide our steps so that we walk with holy hearts and do what is good and pleasing to you"[126] and to our rulers.

Yes, Master, "turn your radiant face toward us"[127] in peace, for our good, that we may be shielded by your powerful hand and rescued from every sin by your uplifted arm. Deliver us, too, from all who hate us without good reason. Give us and all who live on the earth harmony and peace, just as you did to our fathers when they reverently "called upon you in faith and truth."[128] And grant that we may be obedient to your almighty and glorious name, and to our rulers and governors on earth.

**61** You, Master, gave them imperial power through your majestic and indescribable might, so that we, recognizing it was you who gave them the glory and honor, might submit to them, and in no way oppose your will. Grant them, Lord, health, peace, harmony, and stability, so that they may give no offense in administering the government you have given them. For it is you, Master, the heavenly "King of eternity,"[129] who give the sons of men glory and honor and authority over the earth's people. Direct their plans, O Lord, in accord with what is good and pleasing to you, so that they may administer the authority you have given them, with peace, considerateness, and reverence, and so win your mercy. We praise you, who alone are able to do this and still better things for us, through the high priest and guardian of our souls, Jesus Christ. Through him be the glory and the majesty to you now and for all generations and forevermore. Amen.

---

[126] Psalms 39:2; 118:133; 1 Kings 9:4; Deuteronomy 12:25, 28; 13:18; 21:9.

[127] Psalms 66:1; 79:4, 8, 20; Numbers 6:25, 2.

[128] Psalm 144:18; 1 Timothy 2:7.

[129] 1 Timothy 1:17; Tobit 13:6, 10.

**62** We have written enough to you, brothers, about what befits our religion and is most helpful to those who want reverently and uprightly to lead a virtuous life. We have, indeed, touched on every topic – faith, repentance, genuine love, self-control, sobriety, and patience. We have reminded you that you must reverently please almighty God by your uprightness, truthfulness, and long-suffering. You must live in harmony, bearing no grudges, in love, peace, and true considerateness, just as our forefathers, whom we mentioned, won approval by their humble attitude to the Father, God the Creator, and to all men. We were, moreover, all the more delighted to remind you of these things, since we well realized we were writing to people who were real believers and of the highest standing, and who had made a study of the oracles of God's teaching.

**63** Hence it is only right that, confronted with such examples and so many of them, we should bow the neck and adopt the attitude of obedience. Thus, by giving up this futile revolt, we may be free from all reproach and gain the true goal ahead of us. Yes, you will make us exceedingly happy if you prove obedient to what we, prompted by the Holy Spirit, have written, and if, following the plea of our letter for peace and harmony, you rid yourselves of your wicked and passionate rivalry.

We are sending you, moreover, trustworthy and discreet persons who from youth to old age have lived irreproachable lives among us. They will be witnesses to mediate between us. We have done this to let you know that our whole concern has been, and is, to have peace speedily restored among you.

**64** And now may the all-seeing God, the Master of spirits and Lord of all flesh, who chose the Lord Jesus Christ and us through him "to be his own people,"[130] grant to every soul over whom His magnificent and holy name has been invoked,[131] faith, fear, peace, patience, long-suffering, self-control, purity, and sobriety. So may

---

[130] Deuteronomy 14:2.

[131] A reference to the invocation of the Father, Son and Holy Spirit in baptism.

we win his approval through our high priest and defender, Jesus Christ. Through him be glory, majesty, might, and honor to God, now and forevermore. Amen.

**65** Be quick to return our delegates in peace and joy, Claudius Ephebus and Valerius Bito, along with Fortunatus. In that way they will the sooner bring us news of that peace and harmony we have prayed for and so much desire, and we in turn will the more speedily rejoice over your healthy state.

The grace of our Lord Jesus Christ be with you and with all everywhere whom God has called through him. Through him be glory, honor, might, majesty, and eternal dominion to God, from everlasting to everlasting. Amen.

2

# The Didache

## Introduction

In October 1873, theologian (and later Metropolitan of Nicomedia) Philotheos Bryennios made a monumental discovery in the bowels of the library of the Great School of the Nation in Istanbul. He found a complete manuscript of the late first-century catechism known as the *Didachē ton Dōdeka Apostolōn* or "The Teaching of the Twelve Apostles."

This important document had been known by name for many centuries, and it had been quoted in Christian literature, but it was thought to have been lost to history, preserved only in fragments and quotations in other works.

The *Didache* falls into two parts. The first is a code of Christian morals, presented as a choice between the way of life and the way of death. The second part is a manual of church order which lays down some simple rules for the conduct of a rural congregation. It deals with such topics as baptism, the Eucharist, fasting, itinerant prophets, and the local ministry of bishops and deacons. It concludes with a warning paragraph on the approaching end of the world.

### The "Two Ways"

The first part of the *Didache* bears a close relationship to several other early Christian writings. The moral catechism or "Two Ways" of chapters 1 to 5 appears in a rather different version at the end of the Letter of Barnabas (dated between AD 100 and 130), and has also come down to us as an independent document in a Latin translation. Some contend that the "Two Ways" was originally an independent catechism for proselytes, perhaps Jewish in origin, and that it has been incorporated in different forms by the various compilers.

### The Church Order

The second part of the *Didache,* chapters 6 to 15, is a manual of church order. It is assumed that some scribe combined two ancient documents which came into his hands. To the "Two Ways" was appended a late first century set of rules to guide Church life. The writer is familiar with Matthew's Gospel, and quotes Barnabas and the Shepherd of Hermas, as well as books from the Christian Old Testament including Wisdom and Sirach.

## The Teaching of the Twelve Apostles

**1** There are two ways, one of life and one of death; and between the two ways there is a great difference.

Now, this is the way of life: "First, you must love God who made you, and second, your neighbor as yourself."[1] And whatever you want people to refrain from doing to you, you must not do to them.[2]

---

1 Matthew 22:37–39; Leviticus 19:18.

2 *Cf.* Matthew 7:12.

What these maxims teach is this: "Bless those who curse you," and "pray for your enemies." Moreover, fast "for those who persecute you." For "what credit is it to you if you love those who love you? Is that not the way the heathen act?" But you must love those who hate you,[3] and then you will make no enemies. Abstain from carnal passions.[4] If someone strikes you on the right cheek, turn to him the other too, and you will be perfect.[5] If someone forces you to go one mile with him, go along with him for two; if someone robs you of your overcoat, give him your suit as well.[6] If someone deprives you of your property, do not ask for it back.[7] (You could not get it back anyway!) Give to everybody who begs from you, and ask for no return.[8] For the Father wants his own gifts to be universally shared. Happy is the man who gives as the commandment bids him, for he is guiltless! But alas for the man who receives! If he receives because he is in need, he will be guiltless. But if he is not in need he will have to stand trial why he received and for what purpose. He will be thrown into prison and have his action investigated; and "he will not get out until he has paid back the last cent."[9] Indeed, there is a further saying that relates to this: "Let your donation sweat in your hands until you know to whom to give it."[10]

**2** The second commandment of the Teaching: Do not murder; do not commit adultery; do not corrupt boys; do not fornicate; do not steal; do not practice magic; do not go in for sorcery; do not murder a child by abortion or kill a new-born infant. Do not covet your neighbor's property; do not commit perjury; do

---

[3] Matthew 5:44, 46, 47; Luke 6:27, 28, 32, 33.

[4] 1 Peter 2:11.

[5] Matthew 5:39, 48; Luke 6:29.

[6] Matthew 5:40, 41.

[7] Luke 6:30.

[8] *Ibid.*

[9] Matthew 5:26. This whole section 5 should be compared with Hermas, Mand. 2:4–7, on which it is apparently dependent.

[10] Source unknown.

not bear false witness;[11] do not slander; do not bear grudges. Do not be double-minded or double-tongued, for a double tongue is a deadly snare.[12] Your words shall not be dishonest or hollow, but substantiated by action. Do not be greedy or extortionate or hypocritical or malicious or arrogant. Do not plot against your neighbor. Do not hate anybody; but reprove some, pray for others, and still others love more than your own life.

**3** My child, flee from all wickedness and from everything of that sort. Do not be irritable, for anger leads to murder. Do not be jealous or contentious or impetuous, for all this breeds murder.

My child, do not be lustful, for lust leads to fornication. Do not use foul language or leer, for all this breeds adultery.

My child, do not be a diviner, for that leads to idolatry. Do not be an enchanter or an astrologer or a magician. Moreover, have no wish to observe or heed such practices, for all this breeds idolatry.

My child, do not be a liar, for lying leads to theft. Do not be avaricious or vain, for all this breeds thievery.

My child, do not be a grumbler, for grumbling leads to blasphemy. Do not be stubborn or evil-minded, for all this breeds blasphemy.

But be humble, since "the humble will inherit the earth."[13] Be patient, merciful, harmless, quiet, and good; and always have respect for the teaching[14] you have been given. Do not put on airs or give yourself up to presumptuousness. Do not associate with the high and mighty; but be with the upright and humble. Accept whatever happens to you as good, in the realization that nothing occurs apart from God.

---

[11] Exodus 20:13–17; *cf.* Matthew 19:18; 5:33.

[12] Proverbs 21:6.

[13] Psalm 36:11; Matthew 5:5.

[14] Isaiah 66:2.

**4** My child, day and night "you should remember him who preaches God's word to you,"[15] and honor him as you would the Lord. For where the Lord's nature is discussed, there the Lord is. Every day you should seek the company of saints to enjoy their refreshing conversation. You must not start a schism, but reconcile those at strife. "Your judgments must be fair."[16] You must not play favorites when reproving transgressions. You must not be of two minds about your decision.

Do not be one who holds his hand out to take, but shuts it when it comes to giving. If your labor has brought you earnings, pay a ransom for your sins. Do not hesitate to give and do not give with a bad grace; for you will discover who He is that pays you back a reward with a good grace. Do not turn your back on the needy, but share everything with your brother and call nothing your own. For if you have what is eternal in common, how much more should you have what is transient!

Do not neglect your responsibility[17] to your son or your daughter, but from their youth you shall teach them to revere God. Do not be harsh in giving orders to your servants and handmaids. They hope in the same God as you, and the result may be that they cease to revere the God over you both. For when he comes to call us, he will not respect our station, but will call those whom the Spirit has made ready. You servants, for your part, must obey your masters with reverence and fear, as if they represented God.

You must hate all hypocrisy and everything which fails to please the Lord. You must not forsake the Lord's commandments, but observe the ones you have been given, neither adding nor subtracting anything.[18] At the church meeting you must confess your sins, and not approach prayer with a bad conscience. That is the way of life.

---

[15] Hebrews 13:7.

[16] Deuteronomy 1:16, 17; Proverbs 31:9.

[17] Literally, "Do not withhold your hand from . . ."

[18] Deuteronomy 4:2; 12:32.

**5** But the way of death is this: First of all, it is wicked and thoroughly blasphemous: murders, adulteries, lusts, fornications, thefts, idolatries, magic arts, sorceries, robberies, false witness, hypocrisies, duplicity, deceit, arrogance, malice, stubbornness, greediness, filthy talk, jealousy, audacity, haughtiness, boastfulness.[19]

Those who persecute good people, who hate truth, who love lies, who are ignorant of the reward of uprightness, who do not abide by goodness[20] or justice, and are on the alert not for goodness but for evil: gentleness and patience are remote from them. They love vanity,[21] look for profit,[22] have no pity for the poor, do not exert themselves for the oppressed, ignore their Maker, murder children,[23] corrupt the image of God, turn their backs on the needy, oppress the afflicted, defend the rich, unjustly condemn the poor, and are thoroughly wicked. My children, may you be saved from all this!

**6** See that no one leads you astray[24] from this way of the teaching, since such a one's teaching is godless.

If you can bear the Lord's full yoke, you will be perfect. But if you cannot, then do what you can.

Now about food: undertake what you can. But keep strictly away from what is offered to idols, for that implies worshiping dead gods.

**7** Now about baptism: this is how to baptize. Give public instruction on all these points, and then baptize in running water, in the name of the Father and of the Son and of the Holy Spirit.[25] If you do not have running water, baptize in some other. If you

---

19 *Cf.* Matthew 15:19; Mark 7:21, 22; Romans 1:29–31; Galatians 5:19–21.

20 Romans 12:9.

21 Psalm 4:2.

22 Isaiah 1:23.

23 Wisdom 12:6.

24 Matthew 24:4.

25 Matthew 28:19.

cannot in cold, then in warm. If you have neither, then pour water on the head three times, in the name of the Father, Son, and Holy Spirit.[26] Before the baptism, moreover, the one who baptizes and the one being baptized must fast, and any others who can. And you must tell the one being baptized to fast for one or two days beforehand.

**8** Your fasts must not be identical with those of the hypocrites.[27] They fast on Mondays and Thursdays; but you should fast on Wednesdays and Fridays.

You must not pray like the hypocrites,[28] but pray in this manner[29] as the Lord commanded us in his Gospel:

"Our Father in heaven, may your name be hallowed. Let your kingdom come. Let your will be done on earth as it is in heaven. Give us today our daily bread; and forgive us our debts as we forgive our debtors. And do not lead us into temptation but deliver us from the evil one, for yours is the power and the glory forever."

You should pray in this way three times a day.

**9** Now about the Eucharist:[30] This is how to give thanks: First in connection with the cup:[31]

---

[26] *Ibid.*

[27] *I.e.*, the Jews. *Cf.* Matthew 6:16.

[28] Matthew 6:5.

[29] *Cf.* Matthew 6:9–13.

[30] *I.e.*, "the Thanksgiving." The term, however, had become a technical one in Christianity for the special giving of thanks at the Lord's Supper. One might render the verbal form ("give thanks"), which immediately follows, as "say grace, " for it was out of the Jewish forms for grace before and after meals (accompanied in the one instance by the breaking of bread and in the other by sharing a common cup of wine) that the Christian prayers of the Lord's Supper developed.

[31] It is a curious feature of the Didache that the cup has been displaced from the end of the meal to the very beginning.

"We thank you, our Father, for the holy vine[32] of David, your child, which you have revealed through Jesus, your Child.[33] To you be glory forever."

Then in connection with the piece[34] broken off the loaf:

"We thank you, our Father, for the life and knowledge which you have revealed through Jesus, your child. To you be glory forever. As this piece of bread was scattered over the hills[35] and then was brought together and made one, so let your Church be brought together from the ends of the earth into your Kingdom. For yours is the glory and the power through Jesus Christ forever."

You must not let anyone eat or drink of your Eucharist except those baptized in the Lord's name. For in reference to this the Lord said, "Do not give what is sacred to dogs."[36]

**10** After you have finished your meal, give thanks in this way:

"We thank you, holy Father, for your sacred name which you have lodged[37] in our hearts, and for the knowledge and faith and immortality which you have revealed through Jesus, your child. To you be glory forever. Almighty Master, you have created everything[38] for the sake of your name, and have given men food and drink to enjoy that they may thank you. But to us you have given spiritual food and drink and eternal life through Jesus, your

---

32 This may be a metaphorical reference to the divine life and knowledge revealed through Jesus (*cf.* ch. 9). It may also refer to the Messianic promise (*cf.* Isaiah 11:1), or to the Messianic community of the Church (*cf.* Psalm 79:9-10).

33 *Cf.* Acts 4:27. Greek *paīs* has both the meanings *child* and *servant;* it is applied to Christ in light of the Servant passages of Isaiah (42:1–9, 49:1–7, 50:4–9, and 52:13–53:12).

34 An odd phrase, but one that refers to the Jewish custom (taken over in the Christian Eucharist) of grace before meals. The head of the house would distribute to each of the guests a piece of bread broken off a loaf, after uttering the appropriate thanksgiving to God.

35 The reference is likely to the sowing of wheat on the hillsides of Judea.

36 Matthew 7:6.

37 For the phrase *cf.* Nehemiah 1:9.

38 Wisdom 1:14; Sirach 18:1; Revelation 4:11.

child. Above all, we thank you that you are mighty. To you be glory forever.

"Remember, Lord, your Church, to save it from all evil and to make it perfect by your love. Make it holy, and gather it together from the four winds[39] into your Kingdom which you have made ready for it. For yours is the power and the glory forever.

Let grace come and let this world pass away.

Hosanna to the God of David![40]

If anyone is holy, let him come. If not, let him repent.[41]

Our Lord, come![42]

Amen.[43]

In the case of prophets, however, you should let them give thanks in their own way.[44]

**11** Now, you should welcome anyone who comes your way and teaches you all we have been saying. But if the teacher proves himself a renegade and by teaching otherwise contradicts all this, pay no attention to him. But if his teaching furthers the Lord's righteousness and knowledge, welcome him as the Lord.

Now about the apostles and prophets: Act in line with the Gospel precept.[45] Welcome every apostle on arriving, as if he were the Lord. But he must not stay beyond one day. In case of necessity, however, the next day too. If he stays three days, he is a false prophet. On departing, an apostle must not accept anything save sufficient food to carry him till his next lodging. If he asks for money, he is a false prophet.

---

[39] Matthew 24:31.

[40] *Cf.* Matthew 21:9, 15.

[41] Or perhaps "be converted."

[42] *Cf.* 1 Corinthians 16:22.

[43] These terse exclamations may be verses and responses.

[44] *I.e.*, they are not bound by the texts given.

[45] Matthew 10:40, 41.

While a prophet is speaking in the spirit,[46] you must not test or examine him. For "every sin will be forgiven," but this sin "will not be forgiven."[47] However, not everyone who speaks in a spirit is a prophet, but only if he behaves like the Lord. It is by their conduct that the false prophet and the true prophet can be distinguished. For instance, if a prophet marks out a table in the Spirit,[48] he must not eat from it. If he does, he is a false prophet. Again, every prophet who teaches the truth but fails to practice what he preaches is a false prophet. But every attested and genuine prophet who acts with a view to symbolizing the mystery of the Church,[49] and does not teach you to do all he does, must not be judged by you. His judgment rests with God. For the ancient prophets too acted in this way. But if someone says in the Spirit, "Give me money, or something else," you must not heed him. However, if he tells you to give for others in need, no one must condemn him.

**12** Everyone who comes to you in the name of the Lord[50] must be welcomed. Afterward, when you have tested him, you will find out about him, for you have insight into right and wrong. If it is a traveler who arrives, help him all you can. But he must not stay with you more than two days, or, if necessary, three. If he wants to settle with you and is an artisan, he must work for his living. If, however, he has no trade, use your judgment in taking

---

[46] This whole passage (ch. 11:7–12) is a sort of parallel to Matthew 12:31ff. There is an interpretation of the sin against the Holy Ghost, followed by a comment on good and evil conduct (*cf.* Matthew 12:33–37), and concluded by the prophets' signs which are suggested by the sign of the Son of Man (Matthew 22:38 ff.).

[47] Matthew 12:31.

[48] The sense is not clear, but suggests a dramatic portrayal of the Messianic banquet. It was characteristic of the Biblical prophets to drive home their teaching by dramatic and symbolic actions (*cf.* Jeremiah ch. 19; Acts 21:11; etc.).

[49] Literally, "acts with a view to a worldly mystery of the Church." The meaning is not certain, but some dramatic action, symbolizing the mystical marriage of the Church to Christ, is probably intended. The reference may, indeed, be to the prophet's being accompanied by a spiritual sister (*cf.* 1 Corinthians 7:36ff.).

[50] Matthew 21:9; Psalm 117:26; *cf.* John 5:43.

steps for him to live with you as a Christian without being idle. If he refuses to do this, he is trading on Christ. You must be on your guard against such people.

**13** Every genuine prophet who wants to settle with you has a right to his support. Similarly, a genuine teacher himself, just like a workman, has a right to his support.[51] Hence take all the first fruits of vintage and harvest, and of cattle and sheep, and give these first fruits to the prophets. For they are your high priests. If, however, you have no prophet, give them to the poor. If you make bread, take the first fruits and give in accordance with the precept.[52] Similarly, when you open a jar of wine or oil, take the first fruits and give them to the prophets. Indeed, of money, clothes, and of all your possessions, take such first fruits as you think right, and give in accordance with the precept.

**14** On every Lord's Day – his own day[53] – come together and break bread and give thanks, first confessing your sins so that your sacrifice may be pure. Anyone at variance with his neighbor must not join you, until they are reconciled, lest your sacrifice be defiled. For it was of this sacrifice that the Lord said, "Always and everywhere offer me a pure sacrifice; for I am a great King, says the Lord, and my name is marveled at by the nations."[54]

**15** You must, then, elect for yourselves bishops and deacons who are a credit to the Lord, men who are gentle, generous, faithful, and well tried. For their ministry to you is identical with that of the prophets and teachers. Therefore you must not despise them, for along with the prophets and teachers they enjoy a place of honor among you.

---

[51] Matthew 10:10. The provision for the prophet or teacher to settle and to be supported by the congregation implies the birth of the monarchical episcopate. Note the connection of this with the high priesthood (*cf.* Hippolytus, *Apost. Trad.* 3:4) and tithing. No provision is made for the support of the local clergy in ch. 15.

[52] Deuteronomy 18:3–5.

[53] Literally, "On every Lord's Day of the Lord."

[54] Malachi 1:11, 14.

Furthermore, do not reprove each other angrily, but quietly, as you find it in the Gospel. Moreover, if anyone has wronged his neighbor, nobody must speak to him, and he must not hear a word from you, until he repents. Say your prayers, give your charity, and do everything just as you find it in the Gospel of our Lord.

**16** Watch over your life: do not let your lamps go out, and do not keep your loins ungirded; but be ready, for you do not know the hour when our Lord is coming.[55] Meet together frequently in your search for what is good for your souls, since "a lifetime of faith will be of no advantage"[56] to you unless you prove perfect at the very last. For in the final days multitudes of false prophets and seducers will appear. Sheep will turn into wolves, and love into hatred. For with the increase of iniquity men will hate, persecute, and betray each other. And then the world deceiver will appear in the guise of God's Son. He will work signs and wonders[57] and the earth will fall into his hands and he will commit outrages such as have never occurred before. Then mankind will come to the fiery trial and many will fall away[58] and perish, but those who persevere in their faith will be saved[59] by the Curse himself.[60] Then there will appear the signs[61] of the Truth: first the sign of stretched-out hands in heaven,[62] then the sign of a trumpet's blast,[63] and thirdly the resurrection of the dead – though not of all the dead, but as it has been said: "The Lord will come and all his saints with him. Then the world will see the Lord coming on the clouds of heaven."[64]

---

[55] Matthew 24:42, 44; Luke 12:35.

[56] Barnabas 4:9.

[57] Matthew 24:24.

[58] Matthew 24:10.

[59] Matthew 10:22; 24:13.

[60] An obscure reference, but possibly meaning the Christ who suffered the death of one accursed (Galatians 3:13; Barnabas 7:9).

[61] Matthew 24:30.

[62] Another obscure reference, possibly to the belief that the Christ would appear on a glorified cross. *Cf.* Barnabas 12:2–4.

[63] Matthew 24:31.

[64] Zechariah 14:5; 1 Thessalonians 3:13; Matthew 24:30.

3

# Ignatius of Antioch

## Introduction

"A soul seething with the divine *eros.*" This is Chrysostom's description of Ignatius in his eulogy delivered on the martyr's feast in Antioch.[1] It is an apt phrase, for there is a fervor about these letters, an impatience and a heat of excitement in his love for Christ and his expectation of martyrdom.

The significance of these seven letters lies in their being intimacy, familiarity, and popularity. They do not intend to reveal a set of ideas, though they are not lacking in thoughtfulness. Rather they reveal a man. So much of early Christian literature is impersonal that it is refreshing to stumble upon letters reminiscent of the frank and personal note of Paul's correspondence.

The conditions under which Ignatius' letters were written did not make for careful reflection. They are the letters of a prisoner on his way to martyrdom. Their character is popular rather than deep. Their style is compressed and turbulent, reflecting the brusque and impetuous nature of their author, as well as the reality

[1] In *S. Martyrem Ignatium* I, P.G. 50:588.

of a captive subjected to brutality. They disclose a real person, expressing himself in the moment of crisis, and so making clear the intense devotion of his life.

Our knowledge of Ignatius is confined almost entirely to these letters. It is only for the few days when he journeys from Philadelphia to Troas under a military guard that we catch a glimpse of this pastor at the end of the first century. He writes the first four of his letters from Smyrna – three to the churches that had sent delegates, and one to the church at Rome. Pressing northward, he stops again at Troas. From here he writes to the churches of Philadelphia and Smyrna, and adds a personal note to Polycarp. Ignatius was martyred in the Colosseum sometime during the reign of Emperor Trajan (AD 98–117).[2]

Ignatius was bishop of Antioch in Syria.[3] Clement, writing a few decades earlier, was bishop of Rome in the sense of being a chief presbyter in that city; this order is familiar from the New Testament epistles, and from the Didache, and 1 Clement. In these sources, in the mid-first century, the titles "overseer" (*episkopos*) and "elder" (*presbyteros*) are not clearly distinguished. Local assemblies are ruled by bodies of servant-leaders, sometimes called bishops, sometimes presbyters, subject to apostolic figures such as Timothy and Titus who are in turn charged to appoint elders and order the churches under their care.[4] This process had, indeed, already started in the Didache, but in Ignatius it is complete. It is notable that Ignatius does not write to teach or convince his hearers to institute this order; rather, in the face of threatening schisms, he

---

[2] *Cf.* Irenaeus, *Adv. haer.* V. 28:4; Origen and Eusebius, *op. cit.*

[3] According to Origen (Hom. 6 in Luc., P.G. 13, 1814–1815) and Eusebius (*Hist. eccl.* III. 22, 36), the second bishop of Antioch. Eusebius gives Euodius as the first. In his letter to the Romans, Ignatius calls himself "the bishop of Syria," but this doubtless means no more than "the bishop from Syria," "the Syrian bishop." The phrase has no connection with the much later organization of dioceses. In Ignatius' time a bishop was the bishop of a local congregation, not of a far-flung diocese.

[4] Acts 14:23; 1 Timothy 4:4; 2 Timothy 2:2; Titus 1:5

exhorts his readers to love and obey the bishops already in their communities.

Ignatius' other concern is to unmask the heretical movements which are leading to schism. We can gather their main features from his references.

In Philadelphia he came into personal contact with a Judaizing movement similar to the one addressed by Paul in his Letter to the Galatians, and in Revelation 3:9.

At the opposite pole to this error was the Docetic heresy which was rife in Smyrna. Here the attempt to accommodate the Gospel to Greek culture had gone to the limit of denying the reality of the Lord's body. The basic Hellenistic idea that matter was evil led inevitably to disbelief in the incarnation of Christ. God could not have a direct relation with the material world, therefore Christ could not have been genuinely man; he only appeared or seemed to have a body (whence "Docetism," from the Greek *dokeō,* "to seem"). By inventing a sham Christ (a Christ who only "seems" to be), the Docetists prove themselves to be a sham, and are exposed as unreal.

Against these deceptions, Ignatius points to two of the leading emphases of his teaching. One is the divinity of Christ. This foundational understanding was compromised by the Judaizing movement, which viewed Christ as the last of the prophets. There is no confusion for Ignatius: Christ is "our God." He even calls him "Christ God."

The other emphasis of Ignatius' teaching is the reality of Christ's incarnation, passion, and resurrection. He continually stresses the genuine and actual nature of these occurrences and the inseparable unity of flesh and spirit, even after the resurrection. So much so, that such repeated phrases as "in flesh and in spirit" become expressions similar to our "body and soul," and are used as synonyms for "thoroughly" or "completely."

Ignatius clearly knew several letters of Paul. He was most familiar with 1 Corinthians. He likely knew Ephesians; and there may be reminiscences of others. He rarely quotes from the Gospels, though he uses phrases and ideas from Matthew and John. These can be explained by Ignatius' living memory of the apostles and the common apostolic tradition.

## The Letter of Ignatius, Bishop of Antioch, to the Smyrnaeans

### Introduction

Written from Smyrna, where Ignatius and his military guard halted on their way to Rome via the northern road to Troas, this is the longest of Ignatius' letters. Four delegates from the neighboring Ephesian church, including their bishop Onesimus, had been sent to greet and encourage the Ignatius. One of them, the deacon Burrhus, afterward accompanied Ignatius as far as Troas, and perhaps acted as his scribe.

Ignatius takes the occasion to thank the Ephesians for their kindness. While praising them for their unity and orthodoxy, he goes on to warn them against schism and the prevalent Docetic heresy.

### To the Church at Ephesus

Heartiest greetings of pure joy in Jesus Christ from Ignatius, the God-bearer,[5] to the church at Ephesus in Asia.[6] Out of the fullness of God the Father you have been blessed with large numbers and are predestined from eternity to enjoy forever continual and

---

[5] Theophoros, literally "God-bearer." It is probably not a proper name but an epithet indicating his prophetic gifts. He is "full of God" (*cf.* Magnesians, ch. 14).

[6] Ephesus, the scene of Paul's mission and traditionally of John's later activity, was the capital of the Roman province of Asia. It was also the central port of the trade route which joined the Aegean with the East. Hence the reference in ch. 12.

unfading glory. The source of your unity and election is genuine suffering which you undergo by the will of the Father and of Jesus Christ, our God. Hence you deserve to be considered happy.

**1** I gave a godly welcome to your church which has so endeared itself to us by reason of your upright nature, marked as it is by faith in Jesus Christ, our Savior, and by love of him. You are imitators of God; and it was God's blood that stirred you up once more to do the sort of thing you do naturally and have now done to perfection. For you were all zeal to visit me when you heard that I was being shipped as a prisoner from Syria for the sake of our common Name[7] and hope. I hope, indeed, by your prayers to have the good fortune to fight with wild beasts in Rome, so that by doing this I can be a real disciple. In God's name, therefore, I received your large congregation in the person of Onesimus, your bishop in this world,[8] a man whose love is beyond words. My prayer is that you should love him in the spirit of Jesus Christ and all be like him. Blessed is he who let you have such a bishop. You deserved it.

**2** Now about my fellow slave Burrhus[9], your godly deacon, who has been richly blessed. I very much want him to stay with me. He will thus bring honor on you and the bishop. Crocus too, who is a credit both to God and to you, and whom I received as a model of your love, altogether raised my spirits (May the Father of Jesus Christ grant him a similar comfort!), as did Onesimus, Burrhus, Euplus, and Fronto. In them I saw and loved you all. May I always be glad about you, that is, if I deserve to be! It is right, then, for you to render all glory to Jesus Christ, seeing he has glorified you. Thus, united in your submission, and subject to the bishop and the presbytery, you will be real saints.

**3** I do not give you orders as if I were somebody important. For even if I am a prisoner for the Name, I have not yet reached

---

7 *I.e.*, the name of "Christian."

8 In contrast to their heavenly bishop, Christ.

9 A Pauline reminiscence. All Christians are slaves of Christ.

Christian perfection. I am only beginning to be a disciple, so I address you as my fellow students. I needed your coaching in faith, encouragement, endurance, and patience. But since love forbids me to keep silent about you, I hasten to urge you to harmonize your actions with God's mind. For Jesus Christ – that life from which we can't be torn – is the Father's mind, as the bishops too, appointed the world over, reflect the mind of Jesus Christ.

**4** Hence you should act in accord with the bishop's mind, as you surely do. Your presbytery, indeed, which deserves its name and is a credit to God, is as closely tied to the bishop as the strings to a harp. Wherefore your accord and harmonious love is a hymn to Jesus Christ. Yes, one and all, you should form yourselves into a choir,[10] so that, in perfect harmony and taking your pitch from God, you may sing in unison and with one voice to the Father through Jesus Christ. Thus he will heed you, and by your good deeds he will recognize you are members of his Son. Therefore you need to abide in irreproachable unity if you really want to be God's members forever.

**5** If in so short a time I could get so close to your bishop – I do not mean in a natural way, but in a spiritual – how much more do I congratulate you on having such intimacy with him as the Church enjoys with Jesus Christ, and Jesus Christ with the Father. That is how unity and harmony come to prevail everywhere. Make no mistake about it. If anyone is not inside the sanctuary,[11] he lacks God's bread.[12] And if the prayer of one or two has great effect, how much more that of the bishop and the whole Church. He who fails to join in your worship shows his arrogance by the very fact of becoming a schismatic. It is written, moreover, "God resists the

---

[10] The many musical metaphors in Ignatius led to the later legend that he had introduced antiphonal singing into the Church (Socrates, *Hist. eccl.*, VI, ch. 8).

[11] The metaphor is taken from that area of the temple in which faithful Jews gathered for the usual sacrifices. It is contrasted with the outer Court of the Gentiles. The point here is that the true Holy Place is the faithful congregation regularly assembled under its bishop.

[12] *Cf.* John 6:33.

proud."[13] Let us, then, heartily avoid resisting the bishop so that we may be subject to God.

**6** The more anyone sees the bishop modestly silent, the more he should revere him. For everyone the Master of the house sends on his business, we ought to receive as the One who sent him. It is clear, then, that we should regard the bishop as the Lord himself. Indeed, Onesimus spoke very highly of your godly conduct, that you were all living by the truth and harboring no sectarianism. Nay, you heed nobody beyond what he has to say truthfully about Jesus Christ.

**7** Some, indeed, have a wicked and deceitful habit of flaunting the Name about, while acting in a way unworthy of God. You must avoid them like wild beasts. For they are mad dogs which bite on the sly. You must be on your guard against them, for it is hard to heal their bite. There is only one Physician – of flesh yet spiritual, born yet unbegotten, God incarnate, genuine life in the midst of death, sprung from Mary as well as God, first subject to suffering then beyond it – Jesus Christ our Lord.[14]

**8** Let no one mislead you, as, indeed, you are not misled, being wholly God's. For when you harbor no dissension that can harass you, then you are indeed living in God's way. A cheap[15] sacrifice I am, but I dedicate myself to you Ephesians – a church forever famous. Carnal people cannot act spiritually,[16] nor spiritual people carnally, just as faith cannot act like unbelief, or unbelief like faith. But even what you do in the flesh you do spiritually. For you do everything in Christ.

---

[13] Proverbs 3:34.

[14] The first of several compact credal statements in Ignatius. While they are stamped with his originality, they doubtless draw on early formulas used in catechetical instruction and baptism.

[15] The term *peripsēma* (scum, filth), which occurs several times in Ignatius, was used of common criminals who were sacrificed in times of adversity to avert the wrath of the gods. Ignatius uses it as an expression of humility and devotion, to refer to his anticipated martyrdom.

[16] *Cf.* Romans 8:5, 8.

**9** I have heard that some strangers came your way with a wicked teaching, but you did not let them sow it among you. You stopped up your ears to prevent admitting what they disseminated. Like stones of God's Temple, ready for a building of God the Father, you are being hoisted up by Jesus Christ, as with a crane (that is the cross), while the rope you use is the Holy Spirit. Your faith is what lifts you up, while love is the way you ascend to God.

You are all taking part in a religious procession,[17] carrying along with you your God, shrine, Christ, and your holy objects, and decked out from head to toe in the commandments of Jesus Christ. I too am enjoying it all, because I can talk with you in a letter, and congratulate you on changing your old way of life and setting your love on God alone.

**10** "Keep on praying"[18] for others too, for there is a chance of their being converted and getting to God. Let them, then, learn from you at least by your actions. Return their bad temper with gentleness; their boasts with humility; their abuse with prayer. In the face of their error, be "steadfast in the faith."[19] Return their violence with mildness and do not be intent on getting your own back. By our patience let us show we are their brothers, intent on imitating the Lord, seeing which of us can be the more wronged, robbed, and despised. Thus no devil's weed will be found among you; but being thoroughly pure and self-controlled, you will remain united to Jesus Christ in body and soul.

**11** The last days are here. So let us humble ourselves and stand in awe of God's patience, lest it turn out to be our condemnation. Either let us fear the wrath to come or let us value the grace we have: one or the other. Only let our lot be genuine life in Jesus Christ. Do not let anything catch your eye besides him, for whom

---

[17] An abrupt change of metaphor, suggested by the building of a temple. This time the reference is to a heathen procession – perhaps in honor of the Ephesian Artemis. The devotees would be in festive attire and would carry small shrines and amulets of the goddess.

[18] 1 Thessalonians 5:17.

[19] Colossians 1:23.

I carry around these chains – my spiritual pearls! Through them I want to rise from the dead by your prayers. May I ever share in these, so that I may be numbered among the Ephesian Christians who, by the might of Jesus Christ, have always been of one mind with the very apostles.

**12** I realize who I am and to whom I am writing. I am a convict; you have been freed. I am in danger; you are safe. You are the route for God's victims.[20] You have been initiated into the Mysteries with Paul, a real saint and martyr, who deserves to be congratulated. When I come to meet God may I follow in his footsteps, who in all his letters[21] mentions your union with Christ Jesus.

**13** Try to gather together more frequently to celebrate God's Eucharist and to praise him. For when you meet with frequency, Satan's powers are overthrown and his destructiveness is undone by the unanimity of your faith. There is nothing better than peace, by which all strife in heaven and earth is done away.

**14** You will not overlook any of this if you have a thorough belief in Jesus Christ and love him. That is the beginning and end of life: faith the beginning and love the end.[22] And when the two are united you have God, and everything else that has to do with real goodness is dependent on them. No one who professes faith falls into sin, nor does one who has learned to love, hate. "The tree is known by its fruit."[23] Similarly, those who profess to be Christ's will be recognized by their actions. For what matters is not a momentary act of professing, but being persistently motivated by faith.

---

[20] Ephesus was located on the route by which criminals from the provinces would be brought to Rome to supply victims for the amphitheater.

[21] An exaggeration of the fact that in several of Paul's letters he refers to Ephesus and Ephesians.

[22] *Cf.* 1 Timothy 1:5.

[23] Matthew 12:33.

**15** It is better to keep quiet and be real, than to chatter and be unreal. It is a good thing to teach, that is, if the teacher practices what he preaches. There was one such Teacher, who "spoke and it was done"[24]; and what he did in silence[25] is worthy of the Father. He who has really grasped what Jesus said can appreciate his silence. Thus he will be perfect: his words will mean action, and his very silence will reveal his character.

The Lord overlooks nothing. Even secrets are open to him. Let us, then, do everything as if he were dwelling in us. Thus we shall be his temples[26] and he will be within us as our God – as he actually is. This will be clear to us just to the extent that we love him rightly.

**16** Make no mistake, my brothers: adulterers will not inherit God's Kingdom.[27] If, then, those who act carnally suffer death, how much more shall those who by wicked teaching corrupt God's faith for which Jesus Christ was crucified. Such a vile creature will go to the unquenchable fire along with anyone who listens to him.

**17** The reason the Lord let the anointing oil be poured on his head was that he might pass on the aroma of incorruption to the Church. Do not be anointed with the foul smell of the teaching of the prince of this world, lest he capture you and rob you of the life ahead of you. Why do we not all come to our senses by accepting God's knowledge, which is Jesus Christ? Why do we stupidly perish, ignoring the gift which the Lord has really sent?

**18** I am giving my life – not that it's worth much![28] – for the cross, which unbelievers find a stumbling block, but which means to us salvation and eternal life. "Where is the wise man? Where is the debater?"[29] Where are the boasts of those supposedly

---

24 Psalm 32:9.

25 *I.e.*, unobtrusively, and with special reference to his silence at his trial.

26 *Cf.* 1 Corinthians 3:16.

27 *Cf.* 1 Corinthians 6:9, 10.

28 See note 11.

29 1 Corinthians 1:20.

intelligent? For our God, Jesus the Christ, was conceived by Mary, in God's plan being sprung both from the seed of David[30] and from the Holy Spirit. He was born and baptized that by his Passion he might sanctify water.

**19** Now, Mary's virginity and her giving birth escaped the notice of the prince of this world, as did the Lord's death – these are three secrets crying to be told, but wrought in God's silence.[31] How, then, were they revealed to the ages? A star[32] shone in heaven brighter than all the stars. Its light was indescribable and its novelty caused amazement. The rest of the stars, along with the sun and the moon, formed a ring around it; yet it outshone them all, and there was bewilderment whence this unique novelty had arisen. As a result all magic lost its power and all witchcraft ceased. Ignorance was done away with, and the ancient kingdom of evil was utterly destroyed, for God was revealing himself as a man, to bring newness of eternal life.[33] What God had prepared was now beginning. Hence everything was in confusion as the destruction of death was being taken in hand.

**20** If Jesus Christ allows me, in answer to your prayers, and if it is his will, I will explain to you more about God's plan in a second letter I intend to write. I have only touched on this plan in reference to the New Man, Jesus Christ, and how it involves believing in him and loving him, and entails his Passion and resurrection. I will do this especially if the Lord shows me that you are all, every one of you, meeting together under the influence of the grace that we owe to the Name,[34] in one faith and in union with Christ, who was "descended from David according to the flesh"[35] and is Son of man and Son of God. At these meetings

---

[30] *Cf.* Romans 1:3.

[31] God's modesty and reserve in the incarnation were something for which Satan was unprepared.

[32] An expansion of the story in Matthew 2:2, and influenced by Genesis 37:9.

[33] *Cf.* Romans 6:4.

[34] *I.e.*, the name of "Christian."

[35] Romans 1:3.

you should heed the bishop and presbytery attentively, and break one loaf, which is the medicine of immortality, and the antidote which wards off death but yields continuous life in union with Jesus Christ.

**21** I am giving my life for you and for those whom you, to God's honor, sent to Smyrna. I am writing to you from there, giving the Lord thanks and embracing Polycarp and you too in my love. Bear me in mind, as Jesus Christ does you. Pray for the church in Syria, from whence I am being sent off to Rome as a prisoner. I am the least of the faithful there – yet I have been privileged to serve God's honor. Farewell in God the Father and in Jesus Christ, our common hope.

## The Letter of Ignatius, Bishop of Antioch, to the Magnesians

### Introduction

Like the Ephesians, the Christians at Magnesia (a town some fifteen miles from Ephesus) sent delegates to greet Ignatius in Smyrna. Among them was their young bishop, Damas. In his letter to them, Ignatius instructs them not to presume on the youthfulness of their bishop, emphasizes the importance of unity and obedience, and warns them against Judaizing errors.

### To the Church at Magnesia

Every good wish in God the Father and in Jesus Christ from Ignatius, the God-bearer, to the church at Magnesia on the Maeander. In Christ Jesus, our Savior, I greet your church which, by reason of its union with him, is blessed with the favor of God the Father.

**1** I was delighted to hear of your well-disciplined and godly love; and hence, impelled by faith in Jesus Christ, I decided to write to you. Privileged as I am to have this distinguished and godly name,[36] I sing the praises of the churches, even while I am a prisoner. I want them to confess that Jesus Christ, our perpetual Life, united flesh with spirit. I want them, too, to unite their faith with love – there is nothing better than that. Above all, I want them to confess the union of Jesus with the Father. If, with him to support us, we put up with all the spite of the prince of this world and manage to escape, we shall get to God.

**2** Yes, I had the good fortune to see you, in the persons of Damas your bishop (he is a credit to God!), and of your worthy presbyters, Bassus and Apollonius, and of my fellow slave, the deacon Zotion. I am delighted with him, because he submits to the bishop as to God's grace, and to the presbytery as to the law of Jesus Christ.

**3** Now, it is not right to presume on the youthfulness of your bishop. You ought to respect him as fully as you respect the authority of God the Father. Your holy presbyters, I know, have not taken unfair advantage of his apparent youthfulness, but in their godly wisdom have deferred to him – nay, rather, not so much to him as to the Father of Jesus Christ, who is everybody's bishop. For the honor, then, of him who loved us, we ought to obey without any dissembling, since the real issue is not that a man misleads a bishop whom he can see, but that he defrauds the One who is invisible. In such a case he must reckon, not with a human being, but with God who knows his secrets.

**4** We have not only to be called Christians, but to **be** Christians. It is the same thing as calling a man a bishop and then doing everything in disregard of him. Such people seem to me to be acting against their conscience, since they do not come to the valid and authorized services.

---

[36] *I.e.*, *Theophorus*, "God-bearer."

**5** Yes, everything is coming to an end, and we stand before this choice – death or life – and everyone will go "to his own place."[37] One might say similarly, there are two coinages, one God's, the other the world's. Each bears its own stamp – unbelievers that of this world; believers, who are spurred by love, the stamp of God the Father through Jesus Christ. And if we do not willingly die in union with his Passion, we do not have his life in us.

**6** I believed, then, that I saw your whole congregation in these people I have mentioned, and I loved you all. Hence I urge you to aim to do everything in godly agreement. Let the bishop preside in God's place, and the presbyters take the place of the apostolic council. And let the deacons, my special favorites, be entrusted with the ministry of Jesus Christ who was with the Father from eternity and has appeared at the end of the world.

Taking, then, the same attitude as God, you should all respect one another. Let no one think of his neighbor in a carnal way; but always love one another in the spirit of Jesus Christ. Do not let there be anything to divide you, but be in accord with the bishop and your leaders. Thus you will be an example and a lesson of incorruptibility.

**7** The Lord did nothing without the Father,[38] either on his own or by the apostles, because he was at one with him; even so you must not do anything apart from the bishop and presbyters. Do not, moreover, try to convince yourselves that anything done on your own is commendable. Only what you do together is right. Hence you must have one prayer, one petition, one mind, one hope, dominated by love and unsullied joy – that means you must have Jesus Christ. You cannot have anything better than that.

Run off – all of you – to one temple of God, as it were, to one altar, to one Jesus Christ, who came forth from one Father, while still remaining one with him, and returned to him.

---

[37] Acts 1:25.

[38] *Cf.* John 5:19, 30; 8:28.

**8** Do not be led astray by wrong views or by outmoded tales[39] that count for nothing. For if we still go on observing Judaism, we admit we never received grace. The divine prophets themselves lived Christ Jesus' way. That is why they were persecuted, for they were inspired by his grace to convince unbelievers that God is one, and that he has revealed himself in his Son Jesus Christ, who is his Word issuing from the silence[40] and who won the complete approval of him who sent him.

**9** Those, then, who lived by ancient practices arrived at a new hope. They ceased to keep the Sabbath and lived by the Lord's Day, on which our life as well as theirs shone forth, thanks to Him and his death, though some deny this.[41] Through this mystery we got our faith, and because of it we stand our ground so as to become disciples of Jesus Christ, our sole teacher. How, then, can we live without him when even the prophets, who were his disciples by the Spirit, awaited him as their teacher? He, then, whom they were rightly expecting, raised them from the dead, when he came.[42]

**10** We must not, then, be impervious to his kindness. Indeed, were he to act as we do, we should at once be done for. Hence, now we are his disciples, we must learn to live like Christians – to be sure, whoever bears any other name does not belong to God. Get rid, then, of the bad yeast[43] – it has grown stale and sour – and be changed into new yeast, that is, into Jesus Christ. Be salted in him, so that none of you go bad, for your smell will give you away. It is monstrous to talk Jesus Christ and to live like a Jew. For Christianity did not come to faith in Judaism, but Judaism

---

[39] The reference is to apocryphal Jewish legends and allegorical interpretations of the Old Testament (*cf.* 1 Timothy 1:4).

[40] The idea is that by the incarnation God broke his silence, *cf.* Ignatius to the Ephesians, ch. 19.

[41] A passing allusion to the other current heresy, Docetism.

[42] *Cf.* Matthew 27:52.

[43] *Cf.* I Corinthians 5:7.

came to faith in Christianity. People of every tongue have come to believe in it, and so been united together in God.[44]

**11** I do not write in this way, my dear friends, because I have heard that any of you are like that. Rather, well aware of my humble position, I want to caution you ahead of time, lest you fall a prey to stupid ideas, and to urge you to be thoroughly convinced of the nativity, passion, and resurrection, which occurred while Pontius Pilate was governor. Yes, all that was actually and assuredly done by Jesus Christ, our Hope. God forbid that any of you should lose it!

**12** I want to be glad about you ever so much – that is, if I deserve to be. For I am a prisoner, and I cannot compare with one of you who are free. I realize that you are not conceited, for you have Jesus Christ within you. And more, I know you are self-conscious when I praise you, just as Scripture says, "The upright man is his own accuser."[45]

**13** Make a real effort, then, to stand firmly by the orders of the Lord and the apostles, so that "whatever you do, you may succeed"[46] in body and soul, in faith and love, in Son, Father, and Spirit, from first to last – along with your most distinguished bishop, your presbytery, that neatly plaited spiritual wreath, and your godly deacons. Defer to the bishop and to one another as Jesus Christ did to the Father in the days of his flesh, and as the apostles did to Christ, to the Father, and to the Spirit. In that way we shall achieve complete unity.

**14** I realize you are full of God. Hence I have counseled you only briefly. Remember me in your prayers, that I may get to God. Remember too the church in Syria – I do not deserve to be called a member of it. To be sure, I need your united and holy prayers and your love, so that the church in Syria may have the privilege of being refreshed by means of your church.

---

44 *Cf.* Isaiah 66:18.

45 Proverbs 18:17 LXX.

46 Psalm 1:3.

**15** The Ephesians greet you from Smyrna. I am writing to you from there. Like you, they came here for God's glory and have revived me considerably, as has Polycarp, the bishop of Smyrna. The other churches also send their greetings to you in honor of Jesus Christ. Farewell – be at one with God, for you possess an unbreakable spirit, which is what Jesus Christ had.

## The Letter of Ignatius, Bishop of Antioch, to the Trallians

### Introduction

The Christians at Tralles (a town seventeen miles east of Magnesia) sent their bishop, Polybius, to greet Ignatius in Smyrna. His letter in response is characteristic. Its leading themes are unity and obedience to the Church leaders in the face of the spreading Docetic heresy. This letter contains several flashes that reveal Ignatius' character. Particularly striking is chapter 4, where he discloses his own impetuous and fervent nature which contrasts with the calm gentleness of Polybius.

### To the Church at Tralles

Hearty greetings in apostolic style,[47] and every good wish from Ignatius, the God-bearer, to the holy church at Tralles in Asia. You are dear to God, the Father of Jesus Christ, elect and a real credit to him, being completely at peace by reason of the Passion of Jesus Christ, who is our Hope, since we shall rise in union with him.

**1** Well do I realize what a character you have – above reproach and steady under strain. It is not just affected, but it comes naturally to you, as I gathered from Polybius, your bishop. By

[47] *I.e.*, in imitation of Paul's inscriptions.

God's will and that of Jesus Christ, he came to me in Smyrna, and so heartily congratulated me on being a prisoner for Jesus Christ that in him I saw your whole congregation. I welcomed, then, your godly good will, which reached me by him, and I gave thanks that I found you, as I heard, to be following God.

**2** For when you obey the bishop as if he were Jesus Christ, then as I see it, you are living not in a merely human fashion but in Jesus Christ's way, who for our sakes suffered death that you might believe in his death and so escape dying yourselves. It is essential, therefore, to act in no way without the bishop, just as you are doing. Rather submit even to the presbytery as to the apostles of Jesus Christ. He is our Hope,[48] and if we live in union with him now, we shall gain eternal life. Those too who are deacons of the Mysteries[49] of Jesus Christ should in every respect be pleasing to all. For they do not serve mere food and drink,[50] but minister to God's Church. They must therefore avoid leaving themselves open to criticism, as they would shun fire.

**3** Correspondingly, everyone must respect the deacons. They represent Jesus Christ, just as the bishop has the role of the Father, and the presbyters are like God's council and the assembly of the apostles. Apart from these there is no Church. I am sure that you agree with me in this.

In your bishop I received the very model of your love, and I have him with me. His very bearing is a great lesson, while his gentleness is most forceful. I imagine even the godless respect him.

While I could write about this matter more sharply, I spare you out of love. Since, too, I am a convict, I have not thought it my place to give you orders like an apostle.

---

[48] *Cf.* I Timothy 1:1.

[49] I Corinthians 4:1.

[50] The reference is primarily to the Eucharist. In Ignatius' time this was still a supper meal, which the deacons served. There is also an allusion to the distribution of charity for which the deacons, under the bishop, were responsible.

**4** God has granted me many an inspiration, but I keep my limits, lest boasting should be my undoing. For what I need most at this point is to be on my guard and not to heed flatterers. Those who tell me – they are my scourge.[51] To be sure, I am ever so eager to be a martyr, but I do not know if I deserve to be. Many people have no notion of my impetuous ambition. Yet it is all the more a struggle for me. What I need is gentleness by which the prince of this world is overthrown.

**5** Am I incapable of writing to you of heavenly things?[52] No, indeed; but I am afraid to harm you, seeing you are mere babes. You must forgive me, but the chances are you could not accept what I have to say and would choke yourselves. Even in my own case, it is not because I am a prisoner and can grasp heavenly mysteries, the ranks of the angels, the array of principalities, things visible and invisible[53] – it is not because of all that that I am a genuine disciple as yet. There is plenty missing, if we are not going to be forsaken by God.

**6** I urge you, therefore – not I, but Jesus Christ's love – use only Christian food. Keep off foreign fare, by which I mean heresy. For those people mingle Jesus Christ with their own teachings just to gain your confidence under false pretenses. It is as if they were giving a deadly poison mixed with honey and wine, with the result that the unsuspecting victim gladly accepts it and drinks down death with fatal pleasure.

**7** Be on your guard, then, against such people. This you will do by not being puffed up and by keeping very close to [our][54] God, Jesus Christ, and the bishop and the apostles' precepts. Inside the sanctuary a man is pure; outside he is impure. That means that

---

[51] What his flatterers said to him is either suppressed by Ignatius from fear of boasting or has fallen out of the text. We might supply, "You are a true martyr."

[52] *Cf.* 1 Corinthians 3:1, 2.

[53] *Cf.* Colossians 1:16.

[54] Text uncertain.

whoever does anything without bishop, presbytery, and deacons does not have a clear conscience.

**8** It is not because I have heard of any such thing in your case that I write thus. No, in my love for you I am warning you beforehand, since I foresee the devil's wiles. Recapture, then, your gentleness, and by faith (that is the Lord's flesh) and by love (that is Jesus Christ's blood) make yourselves new creatures. Let none of you hold anything against his neighbor. Do not give the heathen opportunities whereby God's people should be scoffed at through the stupidity of a few. For, "Woe to him by whose folly my name is scoffed at before any."[55]

**9** Be deaf, then, to any talk that ignores Jesus Christ, of David's lineage, of Mary; who was really born, ate; and drank; was really persecuted under Pontius Pilate; was really crucified and died, in the sight of heaven and earth and the underworld. He was really raised from the dead, for his Father raised him, just as his Father will raise us, who believe on him, through Christ Jesus, apart from whom we have no genuine life.

**10** And if, as some atheists (I mean unbelievers) say, his suffering was a sham (it is really *they* who are a sham!) then why am I a prisoner? Why do I want to fight with wild beasts? In that case I shall die to no purpose. Yes, and I am maligning the Lord too!

**11** Flee, then, these wicked offshoots which produce deadly fruit. If a man taste of it, he dies outright. They are none of the Father's planting.[56] For had they been, they would have shown themselves as branches of the cross, and borne immortal fruit. It is through the cross, by his suffering, that he summons you who are his members. A head cannot be born without limbs, since God stands for unity. It is his nature.

---

[55] Isaiah 52:5.

[56] *Cf.* Matthew 15:13.

**12** From Smyrna I send you my greetings in which the churches of God that are here with me join. They have altogether raised my spirits – yes, completely. My very chains which I carry around for Jesus Christ's sake, in my desire to get to God, exhort you, "Stay united and pray for one another!"

It is right that each one of you and especially the presbyters should encourage the bishop, in honor of the Father, Jesus Christ, and the apostles.

Out of love I want you to heed me, so that my letter will not tell against you. Moreover, pray for me. By God's mercy I need your love if I am going to deserve the fate I long for,[57] and not prove disqualified.[58]

**13** The Smyrnaeans and Ephesians send their greetings with love. Remember the church of Syria in your prayers. I am not worthy to be a member of it: I am the least of their number. Farewell in Jesus Christ. Submit to the bishop as to God's law, and to the presbytery too. All of you, love one another with an undivided heart. My life is given for you, not only now but especially when I shall get to God.[59] I am still in danger. But the Father is faithful: he will answer my prayer and yours because of Jesus Christ. Under his influence may you prove to be spotless.

---

[57] Text and meaning uncertain.

[58] 1 Corinthians 9:27.

[59] *I.e.*, when I am martyred.

# THE LETTER OF IGNATIUS, BISHOP OF ANTIOCH, TO THE ROMANS

## Introduction

Ignatius' final letter from Smyrna is written to the church of Rome. Unlike his other letters, this one is not concerned with questions of heresy and Church unity. Rather is it an intensely personal document. In it he reveals most clearly his own martyr's spirit. On one hand, it is a plea to the Romans not to interfere with the fate in store for him; and on the other hand it reads like a letter to himself to brace him for the coming ordeal. This letter must be read in the light of the fact that Ignatius was tormented by the brutality of his Roman guard (his "ten leopards" as he calls them), and reacted with the freedom of a man who had already given his life away.

## To the Church at Rome

Greetings in Jesus Christ, the Son of the Father, from Ignatius, the God-bearer, to the church that is in charge of affairs in Roman quarters[60] and that the Most High Father and Jesus Christ, his only Son, have magnificently embraced in mercy and love. You have been granted light both by the will of Him who willed all that is, and by virtue of your believing in Jesus Christ, our God, and

---

[60] The Greek is: *prokathētai en topō chōriou Rōmaiōn.* The words *en topō* might conceivably be taken as "in dignity," and the whole clause rendered: "Which has a precedence of dignity over the district of the Romans." Another suggestion has been to read *Christou* for *chōriou:* "Which presides over the district of the Romans in the place of Christ." The most usual rendering has been: "Which presides [has the chief seat] in the district of the region of the Romans." This presents an ambiguity: is the presidency exercised over the whole Church or only over the district in which the Roman church has its seat? The rendering above is modeled on the phrase *ho topos tēs chōras,* which means "the local circumstances of the district." If, then, the Greek text is correct and *topos* has the sense of "local circumstances," the expression, literally rendered, would be: "Which has the chief seat in the local circumstances of the district of the Romans."

of loving him. You are a credit to God: you deserve your renown and are to be congratulated. You deserve praise and success and are privileged to be without blemish. Yes, you rank first in love,[61] being true to Christ's law and stamped with the Father's name.[62] To you, then, sincerest greetings in Jesus Christ, our God, for you cleave to his every commandment, observing not only their letter but their spirit, being permanently filled with God's grace and purged of every stain alien to it.

**1** Since God has answered my prayer to see you godly people, I have gone on to ask for more. I mean, it is as a prisoner for Christ Jesus that I hope to greet you, if indeed it be God's will that I should deserve to meet my end.[63] Things are off to a good start. May I have the good fortune to meet my fate without interference! What I fear is your generosity which may prove detrimental to me. For you can easily do what you want to, whereas it is hard for me to get to God unless you let me alone.

**2** I do not want you to please men, but to please God,[64] just as you are doing. For I shall never again have such a chance to get to God, nor can you, if you keep quiet, get credit for a finer deed. For if you quietly let me alone, people will see God's Word in me. But if you are enamored of my mere body, I shall, on the contrary, be a meaningless noise. Grant me no more than to be a sacrifice for God while there is an altar at hand. Then you can form yourselves into a choir and sing praises to the Father in Jesus Christ that God gave the bishop of Syria the privilege of reaching the sun's setting when he summoned him from its rising. It is a grand thing for my life to set on the world, and for me to be on my way to God, so that I may rise in his presence.

---

61 The Roman church was early renowned for its extensive acts of charity.

62 A reference to the invocation of the Father's name over the Christian in baptism. The implication is that the Christian by sharing the Father's name shares also the Father's generous nature.

63 *I.e.*, martyrdom.

64 *Cf.* 1 Thessalonians 2:4.

**3** You never grudged anyone. You taught others.[65] So I want you to substantiate the lessons that you commanded them to heed. Just pray that I may have strength of soul and body so that I may not only talk about martyrdom, but really want it. It is not that I want merely to be called a Christian, but actually to **be** one. Yes, if I prove to be one, then I can have the name. Then, too, I shall be a convincing Christian only when the world sees me no more. Nothing you can see has real value. Our God Jesus Christ, indeed, has revealed himself more clearly by returning to the Father. The greatness of Christianity lies in its being hated by the world, not in its being convincing to it.

**4** I am corresponding with all the churches and bidding them all realize that I am voluntarily dying for God – if, that is, you do not interfere. I plead with you, do not do me an unseasonable kindness. Let me be fodder for wild beasts – that is how I can get to God. I am God's wheat and I am being ground by the teeth of wild beasts to make a pure loaf for Christ. I would rather that you fawn on the beasts so that they may be my tomb and no scrap of my body be left. Thus, when I have fallen asleep, I shall be a burden to no one. Then I shall be a real disciple of Jesus Christ when the world sees my body no more. Pray Christ for me that by these means I may become God's sacrifice. I do not give you orders like Peter and Paul. They were apostles: I am a convict. They were at liberty: I am still a slave.[66] But if I suffer, I shall be emancipated by Jesus Christ; and united to him, I shall rise to freedom. Even now as a prisoner, I am learning to forgo my own wishes.

**5** All the way from Syria to Rome I am fighting with wild beasts, by land and sea, night and day, chained as I am to ten leopards (I mean to a detachment of soldiers), who only get worse the better you treat them. But by their injustices I am becoming

---

[65] *I.e.*, about martyrdom, Rome being renowned for the martyrdoms of Peter and Paul.

[66] *Cf.* 1 Corinthians 7:22.

a better disciple, "though not for that reason am I acquitted."[67] What a thrill I shall have from the wild beasts that are ready for me! I hope they will make short work of me. I shall coax them on to eat me up at once and not to hold off, as sometimes happens, through fear. And if they are reluctant, I shall force them to it. Forgive me – I know what is good for me. Now is the moment I am beginning to be a disciple. May nothing seen or unseen begrudge me making my way to Jesus Christ. Come fire, cross, battling with wild beasts, wrenching of bones, mangling of limbs, crushing of my whole body, cruel tortures of the devil – only let me get to Jesus Christ!

**6** Neither the wide bounds of earth nor the kingdoms of this world will avail me anything. "I would rather die"[68] and get to Jesus Christ, than reign over the ends of the earth. That is whom I am looking for – the One who died for us. That is whom I want – the One who rose for us. I am going through the pangs of being born. Sympathize with me, my brothers! Do not stand in the way of my coming to life – do not wish death on me. Do not give back to the world one who wants to be God's; do not trick him with material things. Let me get into the clear light and manhood will be mine. Let me imitate the Passion of my God. If anyone has Him in him, let him appreciate what I am longing for, and sympathize with me, realizing what I am going through.

**7** The prince of this world wants to kidnap me and turn aside my godly purpose. None of you, then, who will be there, must abet him. Rather be on my side – that is, on God's. Do not talk Jesus Christ and set your heart on the world. Harbor no envy. If, when I arrive, I make a different plea, pay no attention to me. Rather heed what I am now writing to you. For though alive, it is with a passion for death that I am writing to you. My Desire[69]

---

[67] 1 Corinthians 4:4.

[68] 1 Corinthians 9:15.

[69] A deliberate pun. Ignatius means both that Christ (on whom his love is set) is crucified, and that all earthly passion has been quelled within himself.

has been crucified and there burns in me no passion for material things. There is living water[70] in me, which speaks and says inside me, "Come to the Father." I take no delight in corruptible food or in the dainties of this life. What I want is God's bread,[71] which is the flesh of Christ, who came from David's line[72]; and for drink I want his blood: an immortal love feast indeed!

**8** I do not want to live any more on a human plane. And so it shall be, if you want it to be. Want it, so that you will be wanted! Despite the brevity of my letter, trust my request. Yes, Jesus Christ will clarify it for you and make you see I am really in earnest. He is the guileless mouth by which the Father has spoken truthfully. Pray for me that I reach my goal. I have written prompted, not by human passion, but by God's will. If I suffer, it will be because you favored me. If I am rejected, it will be because you hated me.

**9** Remember the church of Syria in your prayers. In my place they have God for their shepherd. Jesus Christ alone will look after them[73] – he, and your love. I blush to be reckoned among them, for I do not deserve it, being the least of them and an afterthought.[74] Yet by his mercy I shall be something, if, that is, I get to God.

With my heart I greet you; and the churches which have welcomed me, not as a chance passer-by, but in the name of Jesus Christ, send their love. Indeed, even those that did not naturally lie on my route went ahead to prepare my welcome in the different towns.

**10** I am sending this letter to you from Smyrna by those praiseworthy Ephesians.[75] With me, along with many others, is

---

70 *Cf.* John 4:10; 7:38.

71 *Cf.* John 6:33.

72 *Cf.* Romans 1:3.

73 *I.e.*, be their "overseer" or "bishop."

74 Literally, an "untimely birth," a "miscarriage," suggested by 1 Corinthians 15:8.

75 *I.e.*, who will act as postman. It would seem that some of the Ephesian delegation went ahead of Ignatius to Rome.

Crocus – a person very dear to me. I trust you have had word about those who went ahead of me from Syria to Rome for God's glory. Tell them I am nearly there. They are all a credit to God and to you; so you should give them every assistance. I am writing this to you on the twenty-fourth of August. Farewell, and hold out to the end with the patience of Jesus Christ.

## The Letter of Ignatius, Bishop of Antioch, to the Philadelphians

### Introduction

After leaving Smyrna, Ignatius and his guard pressed on to Troas, where they made a halt before crossing by sea to Neapolis. It was from Troas that Ignatius wrote his last three letters. While their themes are the familiar ones of Church unity and heresy, their special importance lies in the fact that they are directed to churches that Ignatius had actually visited.

Two friends of Ignatius, the deacons Philo and Rheus Agathopus, seem to have joined him in Troas after a stay in Philadelphia. They brought news of the church there and of the fact that the dissident element had slighted them and also slandered the martyr. To answer these charges and to unmask the errors of his opponents, Ignatius wrote this letter; one interesting feature is his account of an actual debate he had with the Judaizers.

### To the Church at Philadelphia

Greetings in the blood of Jesus Christ from Ignatius, the God-bearer, to the church of God the Father and the Lord Jesus Christ, which is at Philadelphia in Asia – an object of the divine mercy and firmly knit in godly unity. Yours is a deep, abiding joy in the Passion of our Lord; and by his overflowing mercy you are thoroughly convinced of his resurrection. You are the very personification of eternal and perpetual joy. This is especially true if you are at one with the bishop, and with the presbyters and deacons, who are at his side and who have been appointed by the will of Jesus Christ. By his Holy Spirit and in accordance with his own will he validated their appointment.

**1** I well realize that this bishop of yours does not owe his ministry to his own efforts or to men. Nor is it to flatter his vanity that he holds this office which serves the common good. Rather does he owe it to the love of God the Father and the Lord Jesus Christ. I have been struck by his charming manner. By being silent he can do more than those who chatter. For he is in tune with the commandments as a harp is with its strings.[76] For this reason I bless his godly mind, recognizing its virtue and perfection, and the way he lives in altogether godly composure, free from fitfulness and anger.

**2** Since you are children of the light of truth, flee from schism and false doctrine. Where the Shepherd is, there follow like sheep.[77] For there are many deceiving wolves who, by means of wicked pleasures, capture those who run God's race. In the face of your unity, however, they will not have a chance.

**3** Keep away from bad pasturage. Jesus Christ does not cultivate it since the Father did not plant it.[78] Not that I found schism among you – rather, you had been sifted.[79] As many as are God's and Jesus Christ's, they are on the bishop's side; and as many as repent and enter the unity of the church, they shall be God's, and thus they shall live in Jesus Christ's way. Make no mistake, my brothers, if anyone joins a schismatic, he will not inherit God's

---

[76] The meaning is not altogether clear.

[77] *Cf.* John 10:7ff.

[78] *Cf.* Matthew 15:13.

[79] Literally, "Rather did I find filtering." The idea is that the church had gone through a purge, the heretical element being filtered or sifted out from the genuine Christians.

Kingdom.[80] If anyone walks in the way of heresy, he is out of sympathy with the Passion.

**4** Be careful, then, to observe a single Eucharist.[81] For there is one flesh of our Lord, Jesus Christ, and one cup of his blood that makes us one, and one altar,[82] just as there is one bishop along with the presbytery and the deacons, my fellow slaves. In that way whatever you do is in line with God's will.

**5** My brothers, in my abounding love for you I am overjoyed to put you on your guard – though it is not I, but Jesus Christ. Being a prisoner for his cause makes me the more fearful that I am still far from being perfect.[83] Yet your prayers to God will make me perfect so that I may gain that fate which I have mercifully been allotted, by taking refuge in the Gospel, as in Jesus' flesh, and in the Apostles, as in the presbytery of the Church.[84] And the prophets, let us love them too,[85] because they anticipated the Gospel in their preaching and hoped for and awaited him, and were saved by believing on him. Thus they were in Jesus Christ's unity. Saints they were, and we should love and admire them, seeing that Jesus Christ vouched for them and they form a real part of the Gospel of our common hope.

**6** Now, if anyone preaches Judaism to you,[86] pay no attention to him. For it is better to hear about Christianity from one of the

---

[80] *Cf.* 1 Corinthians 6:9, 10.

[81] The implication is that the group of Judaizers held separate Eucharists, perhaps on Saturday instead of Sunday (*cf.* Magnesians 9:1).

[82] The term "altar" implies that the Eucharistic meal had a sacrificial meaning.

[83] *I.e.*, proximity to martyrdom makes him afraid that his courage will fail him at the crucial hour.

[84] A possible reference to the "Gospel" and the "Apostles" as the two divisions of the Christian writings.

[85] This is an answer to the criticism of the Judaizers that Ignatius was disparaging the Old Testament.

[86] It may be noted that a similar Judaizing movement in Philadelphia is attacked in Rev. 3:9.

circumcision than Judaism from a Gentile.[87] If both, moreover, fail to talk about Jesus Christ, then to me they are tombstones and graves of the dead,[88] on which only human names are inscribed. Flee, then, the wicked tricks and snares of the prince of this world, lest his suggestions wear you down, and you waver in your love. Rather, meet together, all of you, with a single heart. I thank my God that in my relations with you I have nothing to be ashamed of. No one can brag secretly or openly that I was the slightest burden to anyone. I trust, too, that none of those I talked to will need to take what I say as a criticism of them.

**7** Some there may be who wanted in a human way to mislead me, but the Spirit is not misled, seeing it comes from God. For "it knows whence it comes and whither it goes,"[89] and exposes what is secret.[90] When I was with you I cried out, raising my voice – it was God's voice[91] – "Pay heed to the bishop, the presbytery, and the deacons." Some, it is true, suspected that I spoke thus because I had been told in advance that some of you were schismatics. But I swear by Him for whose cause I am a prisoner, that from no human channels did I learn this. It was the Spirit that kept on preaching in these words: "Do nothing apart from the bishop; keep your bodies as if they were God's temple; value unity; flee schism; imitate Jesus Christ as he imitated his Father."

**8** I, then, was doing all I could, as a man utterly devoted to unity. Where there is schism and enmity, God has no place. The Lord forgives all who repent – if, that is, their repentance brings them into God's unity and to the bishop's council. I put my confidence in the grace of Jesus Christ. He will release you from all your chains.[92]

---

[87] Circumcision does not seem to have been included in this Judaizing movement as it had been in Galatia (Galatians 6:12).

[88] *Cf.* Matthew 23:27.

[89] *Cf.* John 3:8.

[90] *Cf.* 1 Corinthians 2:10, 11.

[91] An instance of the "God-bearer's" prophetic utterances.

[92] *Cf.* Isaiah 58:6.

I urge you, do not do things in cliques, but act as Christ's disciples. When I heard some people saying, "If I don't find it in the original documents, I don't believe it in the Gospel," I answered them, "But it *is* written there." They retorted, "That's just the question."[93] To my mind it is Jesus Christ who is the original documents. The inviolable archives are his cross and death and his resurrection and the faith that came by him. It is by these things and through your prayers that I want to be justified.

**9** Priests are a fine thing, but better still is the High Priest[94] who was entrusted with the Holy of Holies. He alone was entrusted with God's secrets. He is the door to the Father.[95] Through it enter Abraham, Isaac, and Jacob, the prophets and apostles and the Church. All these find their place in God's unity. But there is something special about the Gospel – I mean the coming of the Savior, our Lord Jesus Christ, his Passion and Resurrection. The beloved prophets announced his coming; but the Gospel is the crowning achievement forever. All these things, taken together, have their value, provided you hold the faith in love.

**10** Thanks to your prayers and to the love that you have for me in Christ Jesus, news has reached me that the church at Antioch in Syria is at peace.[96] Consequently, it would be wise for you, as a church of God, to elect a deacon to go there on a mission, as God's representative, and at a formal service to congratulate them and

---

[93] The point of the argument is that the Old Testament is the final court of appeal. It constitutes the "original documents" which validate the Gospel. The New Testament, as a book of canonical authority, is still in process of formation. The Bible of the primitive Church is the Septuagint. Hence a point of doctrine turns on the interpretation of Old Testament texts which are viewed as prophetically pointing to Christianity. When, however, an impasse is reached in the argument, Ignatius makes the tradition of the Gospel the final authority. He thus opens himself to the criticism of disparaging the Old Testament (*cf.* chapter 5).

[94] *I.e.*, Jesus Christ. This reflects the theme elaborated in The Epistle to the Hebrews, but Ignatius is not necessarily dependent on it. It must have been a Christian commonplace.

[95] *Cf.* John 10:7, 9.

[96] The first indication that the persecution in Antioch, which led to Ignatius' condemnation, has blown over. The news seems to have reached him at Troas.

glorify the Name. He who is privileged to perform such a ministry will enjoy the blessing of Jesus Christ, and you too will win glory. If you really want to do this for God's honor, it is not impossible, just as some of the churches in the vicinity have already sent bishops; others presbyters and deacons.[97]

**11** Now about Philo, the deacon from Cilicia. He is well spoken of and right now he is helping me in God's cause, along with Rheus Agathopus – a choice person – who followed me from Syria and so has said good-bye to this present life. They speak well of you, and I thank God on your account that you welcomed them, as the Lord does you. I hope that those who slighted them will be redeemed by Jesus Christ's grace. The brothers in Troas send their love and greetings. It is from there that I am sending this letter to you by Burrhus.[98] The Ephesians and Smyrnaeans have done me the honor of sending him to be with me. They in turn will be honored by Jesus Christ, on whom they have set their hope with body, soul, spirit, faith, love, and a single mind. Farewell in Christ Jesus, our common Hope.

## The Letter of Ignatius, Bishop of Antioch, to the Smyrnaeans

### Introduction

At Smyrna Ignatius had come into personal contact with Docetism. To his mind this presented such an imminent danger to the church there that his letter plunges at once into the theme with a vigorous affirmation of the reality of Christ's Passion and resurrection. Only toward the end of his letter does he refer to

---

[97] An indication of the deep sense of solidarity that bound together the widely scattered Christian congregations.

[98] The Greek is ambiguous. Burrhus might be either postman or secretary.

the hospitality he had received during his stay. The number of greetings at the conclusion indicate the warm welcome he had been given.

Another interesting feature of this letter is the first appearance in Christian literature of the phrase "the catholic Church" (chapter 8). The word stands for the Church complete in itself, universal and transcendent, distinct from the local assembly.

### To the Church at Smyrna

Heartiest greetings in all sincerity and in God's Word from Ignatius, the God-bearer, to the church of God the Father and the beloved Jesus Christ, which is at Smyrna in Asia. By God's mercy you have received every gift; you abound in faith and love, and are lacking in no gift.[99] You are a wonderful credit to God and real saints.[100]

**1** I extol Jesus Christ, the God who has granted you such wisdom. For I detected that you were fitted out with an unshakable faith, being nailed, as it were, body and soul to the cross of the Lord Jesus Christ, and being rooted in love by the blood of Christ. Regarding our Lord, you are absolutely convinced that on the human side he was actually sprung from David's line,[101] Son of God according to God's will and power, actually born of a virgin, baptized by John, that "all righteousness might be fulfilled by him,"[102] and actually crucified for us in the flesh, under Pontius Pilate and Herod the Tetrarch. (We are part of His fruit which grew out of his most blessed Passion.)[103] And thus, by his resurrection,

---

[99] *Cf.* 1 Corinthians 1:7.

[100] The word literally means "bearer of sacred objects," and is taken from heathen ceremonial; *cf.* Ignatius to the Ephesians ch. 9. The sacred objects here would be their virtues.

[101] *Cf.* Romans 1:3.

[102] *Cf.* Matthew 3:15.

[103] Ignatius changes his metaphors: The cross here is a tree; in the next sentence it is a military rallying standard.

he raised a standard[104] to rally his saints and faithful forever – whether Jews or Gentiles – in one body of his Church.[105]

**2** For it was for our sakes that he suffered all this, to save us. And he genuinely suffered, as even he genuinely raised himself. It is not as some unbelievers say, that his Passion was a sham. It is they who are a sham! Yes, and their fate will fit their fantasies – they will be ghosts and apparitions.

**3** For myself, I am convinced and believe that even after the resurrection he was in the flesh. Indeed, when he came to Peter and his friends, he said to them, "Take hold of me, touch me and see that I am not a bodiless ghost."[106] And they at once touched him and were convinced, clutching his body and his very breath. For this reason they despised death itself, and proved victors over it. Moreover, after the resurrection he ate and drank with them[107] as a real human being, although in spirit he was united with the Father.

**4** I urge these things on you, my friends, although I am well aware that you agree with me. But I warn you in advance against wild beasts in human shapes. You must not only refuse to receive them, but if possible, you must avoid meeting them. Just pray for them that they may somehow repent, hard as that is. Yet Jesus Christ, our genuine life, has the power to bring it about. If what our Lord did is a sham, so is my being in chains. Why, then, have I given myself up completely to death, fire, sword, and wild beasts? For the simple reason that near the sword means near God. To be with wild beasts means to be with God. But it must all be in the name of Jesus Christ. To share in his Passion I go through

---

104 *Cf.* Isaiah 5:26; 11:12.

105 *Cf.* Ephesians 2:16.

106 A possible allusion to Luke 24:39. The latter part of the saying occurs in *The Preaching of Peter* and in *The Gospel According to the Hebrews.*

107 *Cf.* Acts 10:41.

everything, for he who became the perfect man gives me the strength.[108]

**5** Yet in their ignorance some deny him – or rather have been denied by him, since they advocate death rather than the truth. The prophets and the law of Moses have failed to convince them – nay, to this very day the Gospel and the sufferings of each one of us have also failed, for they class our sufferings with Christ's.[109] What good does anyone do me by praising me and then reviling my Lord by refusing to acknowledge that he carried around live flesh? He who denies this has completely disavowed him and carries a corpse around. The names of these people, seeing they are unbelievers, I am not going to write down. No, far be it from me even to recall them until they repent and acknowledge the Passion, which means our resurrection.

**6** Let no one be misled: heavenly beings, the splendor of angels, and principalities, visible and invisible, if they fail to believe in Christ's blood, they too are doomed. "Let him accept it who can."[110] Let no one's position swell his head, for faith and love are everything – there is nothing preferable to them.

Pay close attention to those who have wrong notions about the grace of Jesus Christ, which has come to us, and note how at variance they are with God's mind. They care nothing about love: they have no concern for widows or orphans, for the oppressed, for those in prison or released, for the hungry or the thirsty.

**7** They hold aloof from the Eucharist and from services of prayer, because they refuse to admit that the Eucharist is the flesh of our Savior Jesus Christ,[111] which suffered for our sins and

---

108 *Cf.* Philippians 4:13.

109 Literally, "They have the same idea about us." The sense would seem to be that Christian martyrdom is meaningless as an imitation of the Christ if he never really suffered.

110 Matthew 19:12.

111 It is not clear whether the Docetists abandoned the Eucharistic rite altogether, or whether they held separate Eucharists, giving them a different meaning to suit their views.

which, in his goodness, the Father raised. Consequently those who wrangle and dispute God's gift face death. They would have done better to love and so share in the resurrection. The right thing to do, then, is to avoid such people and to talk about them neither in private nor in public. Rather pay attention to the prophets and above all to the Gospel. There we get a clear picture of the Passion and see that the resurrection has really happened.

**8** Flee from schism as the source of mischief. See that you all follow the bishop as Jesus Christ does the Father. Follow, too, the presbytery as you would the apostles; and respect the deacons as you would God's law. Nobody must do anything that has to do with the Church without the bishop's approval. You should regard that Eucharist as valid which is celebrated either by the bishop or by someone he authorizes. Where the bishop is present, there let the congregation gather, just as where Jesus Christ is, there is the catholic Church. Without the bishop's supervision, no baptisms or love feasts are permitted. On the other hand, whatever he approves pleases God as well. In that way everything you do will be on the safe side and valid.

**9** It is well for us to come to our senses at last, while we still have a chance to repent and turn to God. It is a fine thing to acknowledge God and the bishop. He who pays the bishop honor has been honored by God. But he who acts without the bishop's knowledge is in the devil's service.

By God's grace may you have an abundance of everything! You deserve it. You have brought me no end of comfort; may Jesus Christ do the same for you! Whether I was absent or present, you gave me your love. May God requite you! If for his sake you endure everything, you will get to him.

**10** It was good of you to welcome Philo and Rheus Agathopus as deacons of the Christ God. They accompanied me in God's cause, and they thank the Lord on your behalf that you provided them every comfort. I can assure you, you will lose nothing by it. Prisoner as I am, I am giving my life for you – not that it's worth much! You did not scorn my chains and were not ashamed of them.[112] Neither will Jesus Christ be ashamed of you. You can trust him implicitly!

**11** Your prayers have reached out as far as the church at Antioch in Syria. From there I have come, chained with these magnificent chains, and I send you all greetings. I do not, of course, deserve to be a member of that church, seeing I am the least among them. Yet it was God's will to give me the privilege – not, indeed, for anything I had done of my own accord, but by his grace. Oh, I want that grace to be given me in full measure, that by your prayers I may get to God! Well, then, so that your own conduct may be perfect on earth and in heaven, it is right that your church should honor God by sending a delegate in his name to go to Syria and to congratulate them on being at peace, on recovering their original numbers, and on having their own corporate life restored to them. To my mind that is what God would want you to do: to send one of your number with a letter, and thus join with them in extolling the calm which God has granted them, and the fact that they have already reached a haven, thanks to your prayers. Seeing you are perfect, your intentions must be perfect as well.[113] Indeed, if you want to do what is right, God stands ready to give you his help.

**12** The brothers in Troas send their love to you. From there I am sending this letter to you by Burrhus. You joined with your Ephesian brothers in sending him to be with me, and he has altogether raised my spirits. I wish everyone would be like him, since he is a model of what God's ministry should be. God's grace will repay him for all he has done for me. Greetings to your bishop[114] (he is such a credit to God!), and to your splendid presbytery and to my fellow slaves the deacons, and to you all, every one of you, in Jesus Christ's name, in his flesh and blood, in his Passion and resurrection, both bodily and spiritual, and in

---

[112] *Cf.* 2 Timothy 1:16.

[113] *Cf.* Philemon 3:15.

[114] *I.e.*, Polycarp, to whom the following letter is addressed.

unity – both God's and yours. Grace be yours, and mercy, peace, and endurance, forever.

**13** Greetings to the families of my brothers, along with their wives and children, and to the virgins enrolled with the widows.[115] I bid you farewell in the Father's power. Philo, who is with me, sends you greetings. Greetings to Tavia's family. I want her to be firmly and thoroughly grounded in faith and love. Greetings to Alce, who means a great deal to me, and to the inimitable Daphnus and to Eutecnus and to each one of you. Farewell in God's grace.

## The Letter of Ignatius, Bishop of Antioch, to Polycarp

### Introduction

Along with the letter to the church of Smyrna, Ignatius wrote to Smyrna's bishop, Polycarp. One of the most distinguished figures of the early Church, who crowned his own old age with martyrdom, Polycarp had given Ignatius a generous welcome, as the latter mentions in other letters. This is an intimate and personal letter – the shortest of them all. Polycarp was the younger of the two men, perhaps in his early forties, and Ignatius is characteristically forthright in his advice.

The sense of Christian solidarity which bound together the local churches is evident from the various delegations which Ignatius received in Smyrna. The suggestion, however, in the letter to the Philadelphians and repeated in this one to Polycarp, that the churches should send delegates as far as Syrian Antioch to congratulate the Christians on the cessation of persecution, is a telling witness to the common spirit of the local congregations.

[115] The meaning is not altogether clear. It appears, however, that the order of widows, established for works of charity (*cf.* 1 Timothy 5:9), sometimes included virgins.

In a day when travel was neither easy nor free from danger, the dispatching of such messengers reflects the deep unity of the Christian brotherhood.

## To Polycarp, bishop of Smyrna

Heartiest greetings from Ignatius, the God-bearer, to Polycarp, who is bishop of the church at Smyrna – or rather who has God the Father and the Lord Jesus Christ for his bishop.

**1** While I was impressed with your godly mind, which is fixed, as it were, on an immovable rock, I am more than grateful that I was granted the sight of your holy face. God grant I may never forget it! By the grace which you have put on, I urge you to press forward in your race and to urge everybody to be saved. Vindicate your position by giving your whole attention to its material and spiritual sides.[116] Make unity your concern – there is nothing better than that. Lend everybody a hand, as the Lord does you. "Out of love be patient"[117] with everyone, as indeed you are. Devote yourself to continual prayer. Ask for increasing insight. Be ever on the watch by keeping your spirit alert. Take a personal interest in those you talk to, just as God does. "Bear the infirmities"[118] of everyone, like an athlete in perfect form. The greater the toil, the greater the gain.

**2** It is no credit to you if you are fond of good pupils. Rather by your gentleness subdue those who are annoying. Not every wound is healed by the same plaster. Relieve spasms of pain with poultices. In all circumstances be "wise as a serpent," and perpetually "harmless as a dove."[119] The reason you have a body as

---

[116] The reference is to the double nature of the episcopal office in the Early Church. The bishop was at once the guardian of the common chest fund for the needy and the spiritual father of his congregation.

[117] Ephesians 4:2.

[118] Matthew 8:17.

[119] Matthew 10:16.

well as a soul is that you may win the favor of the visible world.[120] But ask that you may have revelations of what is unseen. In that way you will lack nothing and have an abundance of every gift.

Just as pilots demand winds and a storm-tossed sailor a harbor, so times like these demand a person like you. With your help we will get to God. As God's athlete, be sober. The prize, as you very well know, is immortality and eternal life. Bound as I am with chains that you kissed,[121] I give my whole self for you – cheap sacrifice though it is!

**3** You must not be panic-stricken by those who have an air of credibility but who teach heresy.[122] Stand your ground like an anvil under the hammer. A great athlete must suffer blows to conquer. And especially for God's sake must we put up with everything, so that he will put up with us. Show more enthusiasm than you do. Mark the times. Be on the alert for him who is above time, the Timeless, the Unseen, the One who became visible for our sakes, who was beyond touch and passion, yet who for our sakes became subject to suffering, and endured everything for us.

**4** Widows must not be neglected. After the Lord, you must be their protector. Do not let anything be done without your consent; and do not do anything without God's, as indeed you do not. Stand firm. Hold services more often. Seek out everybody by name. Do not treat slaves and slave girls contemptuously.[123] Neither must they grow insolent. But for God's glory they must give more devoted service, so that they may obtain from God a better freedom. Moreover, they must not be overanxious to gain

---

[120] The idea would seem to be that having a body leads one to seek a proper harmony with all persons and things belonging to the material world. This sentiment is the opposite of the Docetic belief, which saw in matter the source of evil.

[121] It is possible that the faithful kissed the chains of the martyr, though a more general sense ("the chains which you did not despise and in which you delighted") may be intended.

[122] *Cf.* 1 Timothy 1:3; 6:3.

[123] *Cf.* 1 Timothy 6:2.

their freedom at the community's expense, lest they prove to be slaves of selfish passion.

**5** Flee from such wicked practices – nay, rather, preach against them.

Tell my sisters to love the Lord and to be altogether contented with their husbands. Similarly urge my brothers in the name of Jesus Christ "to love their wives as the Lord loves the Church."[124] If anyone can live in chastity for the honor of the Lord's flesh, let him do so without ever boasting. If he boasts of it, he is lost; and if he is more highly honored than the bishop, his chastity is as good as forfeited. It is right for men and women who marry to be united with the bishop's approval. In that way their marriage will follow God's will and not the promptings of lust. Let everything be done so as to advance God's honor.

**6** Pay attention to the bishop so that God will pay attention to you. I give my life as a sacrifice (poor as it is) for those who are obedient to the bishop, the presbyters, and the deacons. Along with them may I get my share of God's reward! Share your hard training together – wrestle together, run together, suffer together, go to bed together, get up together, as God's stewards, assessors, and assistants. Give satisfaction to Him in whose ranks you serve and from whom you get your pay.[125] Let none of you prove a deserter. Let your baptism be your arms; your faith, your helmet; your love, your spear; your endurance, your armor.[126] Let your deeds be your deposits, so that you will eventually get back considerable savings.[127] Be patient, then, and gentle with each other, as God is with you. May I always be happy about you!

---

[124] Ephesians 5:25, 29.

[125] *Cf.* 2 Timothy 2:4.

[126] *Cf.* Ephesians 6:11–17.

[127] The metaphor is taken from the custom of withholding from soldiers a part of their wages and depositing it in a savings bank, from which they were paid on their discharge. The military metaphors in this passage, and the curious number of Latin words, are likely due to the fact that Ignatius had a guard of ten Roman soldiers.

**7** News has reached me that, thanks to your prayers, the church at Antioch in Syria is now at peace. At this I have taken new courage and, relying on God, I have set my mind at rest – assuming, that is, I may get to God through suffering, and at the resurrection prove to be your disciple. So, my dear Polycarp (and how richly God has blessed you!), you ought to call a most religious council and appoint somebody whom you regard as especially dear and diligent, and who can act as God's messenger. You should give him the privilege of going to Syria and of advancing God's glory by extolling your untiring generosity. A Christian does not control his own life, but gives his whole time to God. This is God's work, and when you have completed it, it will be yours as well. For God's grace gives me confidence that you are ready to act generously when it comes to his business. It is because I am well aware of your earnest sincerity that I limit my appeal to so few words.

**8** I have been unable to write to all the churches because I am sailing at once (so God has willed it) from Troas to Neapolis. I want you, therefore, as one who has the mind of God, to write to the churches ahead and to bid them to do the same. Those who can should send representatives, while the others should send letters by your own delegates. In that way you will win renown, such as you deserve, by an act that will be remembered forever.

Greetings to every one of you personally, and to the widow of Epitropus[128] with her children and her whole family. Greetings to my dear Attalus. Greetings to the one who is to be chosen to go to Syria. Grace will ever be with him and with Polycarp who sends him. I bid you farewell as always in our God, Jesus Christ. May you abide in him and so share in the divine unity and be under God's care. Greetings to Alce, who means a great deal to me. Farewell in the Lord.

---

[128] It is possible that Epitropus is not a proper name but a title, so that the phrase means "the widow of the procurator."

4

# Polycarp of Smyrna

At the time of his martyrdom, Polycarp, the bishop of Smyrna, confessed that he had been a Christian for eighty-six years. Since the date of his martyrdom can be fixed with reasonable certainty as occurring in A.D. 155 or 156, his birth could therefore not have been later than the year 69 or 70. This makes him perhaps forty years of age when he visited and corresponded with Ignatius on the latter's way to martyrdom in Rome.

Polycarp's life spanned that critical era of the Church's development following the passing of the apostles, and encompassed the menacing growth of state persecution, the Docetic and Gnostic heresies, and the coalescence of the canon of New Testament writings.

## Letter of Polycarp, Bishop of Smyrna, to the Philippians

### Introduction

Brief as it is, Polycarp's letter gives us the measure of the man. He was simple, humble, and direct. There was nothing subtle or pretentious about him. He does not appear to have had much in the way of formal education. His Greek is without style, without the faintest touch of rhetoric, without learned allusion. He is not versed, as he himself admitted, in the Scriptures, i.e., the Old Testament. But he had meditated much on Christian writings; his letter is a veritable mosaic of quotation and allusion to them. He shows familiarity with Matthew's Gospel, the Acts of the Apostles, the letters of Paul, and 1 Peter, and also quotes often from 1 Clement.

Modern critics are fond of calling him "unoriginal." It is true; he shows not the slightest interest in theological or philosophical speculation. He never argues with heresy, but treats it uncompromisingly with disdain and contempt. Any deviation from the norm of "the faith once delivered" provokes him to strong language. Yet if he appears harsh and unyielding with offenders against the truth as he has received it, Polycarp can be gentle and compassionate with human failings in the moral order – as in the case, for example, of the presbyter Valens.[1] He had the insight and the method, as it were instinctively, of the true pastor of souls. And the simplicity and honesty of his own character won him the veneration of his church and the respect of the heathen populace of Smyrna.

## To the Church at Philippi

Polycarp and the presbyters with him, to the church of God that sojourns at Philippi; may mercy and peace be multiplied to you from God Almighty and Jesus Christ, our Savior.[2]

**1** I rejoice with you greatly in our Lord[3] Jesus Christ, in that you have welcomed the models of true Love,[4] and have helped

---

[1] *Cf.* ch. 11.

[2] I Peter 1:1, 2; Jude 2.

[3] Philippians 4:10; 2:17.

[4] The Love, of whom the martyrs are models, may refer either to Christ or to all those who love God and their neighbor. *Cf.* 1 John 4:16; Ignatius to the Romans ch. 6, 7.

on their way,[5] as opportunity was given you, those men who are bound in fetters which become the saints,[6] which are indeed the diadems of the true elect of God and of our Lord. And I also rejoice because the firm root of your faith, famous from the earliest times,[7] still abides and bears fruit for our Lord Jesus Christ, who endured for our sins even to face death, "whom God raised up, having loosed the pangs of Hades."[8] In him, "though you have not seen him, you believe with joy unspeakable and full of glory"[9] – joy that many have longed to experience – knowing that "you are saved by grace, not because of works,"[10] namely, by the will of God through Jesus Christ.

**2** "Therefore, girding your loins, serve God in fear" and in truth,[11] forsaking empty talkativeness and the erroneous teaching of the crowd,[12] "believing on him who raised our Lord Jesus Christ from the dead and gave him glory"[13] and a throne on his right hand; "to whom he subjected all things, whether in heaven or on earth,"[14] whom "everything that breathes"[15] serves, who will come as "judge of the living and the dead,"[16] whose blood God will require from those who disobey him.[17] For "he who raised him from the dead will raise us also,"[18] if we do his will and follow his commandments, and love what he loved,[19] refraining from all

---

5 Acts 15:3.

6 Smyrnaeans ch. 11.

7 Acts 15:7; Colossians 1:6.

8 Acts 2:24 (Western text).

9 1 Peter 1:8.

10 Ephesians 2:5, 8, 9.

11 1 Peter 1:13; Ephesians 6:14; Psalm 2:11; *cf.* 1 Clement 19:1.

12 1 Timothy 1:6; 1 Clement 9:1; 7:2; Ignatius to the Philippians 1:1.

13 1 Peter 1:21.

14 Philippians 3:21; 2:10; 1 Corinthians 15:28.

15 Psalm 150:6; Isaiah 57:16.

16 Acts 10:42.

17 Ezekiel 3:18; Luke 11:50, 51.

18 2 Corinthians 4:14; 1 Corinthians 6:14; Romans 8:11.

19 1 John 4:11, 12.

wrongdoing, avarice, love of money, slander, and false witness; "not returning evil for evil or abuse for abuse,"[20] or blow for blow, or curse for curse; but rather remembering what the Lord said when he taught: "Judge not, that you be not judged; forgive, and you will be forgiven; be merciful, that you may be shown mercy; the measure you give will be the measure you get"[21];and "blessed are the poor and those persecuted for righteousness' sake, for theirs is the Kingdom of God."[22]

**3** I write these things about righteousness, brethren, not at my own instance, but because you first invited me to do so. Certainly, neither I nor anyone like me can follow the wisdom of the blessed and glorious Paul, who, when he was present among you face to face with the generation of his time,[23] taught you accurately and firmly "the word of truth."[24] Also when absent he wrote you letters that will enable you, if you study them carefully,[25] to grow in the faith delivered to you – "which is a mother of us all," accompanied by hope, and led by love to God and Christ and our neighbor.[26] For if anyone is occupied in these, he has fulfilled the commandment of righteousness; for he who possesses love is far from all sin.

**4** But "the love of money is the beginning of all evils."[27] Knowing, therefore, that "we brought nothing into the world, and we cannot take anything out,"[28] let us arm ourselves "with the weapons of righteousness,"[29] and let us first of all teach ourselves to live by the commandment of the Lord.

---

20 1 Peter 3:9.

21 Matthew 7:1, 2; Luke 6:36–38; *cf.* 1 Clement 13:2.

22 Luke 6:20; Matthew 5:3, 10.

23 Acts 16:12, 13.

24 Ephesians 1:13.

25 *Cf.* 1 Clement ch. 45.

26 Colossians 1:4, 5; *cf.* 1 Thessalonians 1:4 for the order: faith, love, hope.

27 1 Timothy 6:10.

28 1 Timothy 6:7; *cf.* Job 1:21.

29 2 Cor. 6:7.

Then you must teach your wives in the faith delivered to them and in love and purity – to cherish their own husbands[30] in all fidelity, and to love all others equally in all chastity, and to educate their children in the fear of God.[31] And the widows should be discreet in their faith pledged to the Lord, praying unceasingly on behalf of all,[32] refraining from all slander, gossip, false witness, love of money – in fact, from evil of any kind – knowing that they are God's altar, that everything is examined for blemishes,[33] and nothing escapes him whether of thoughts or sentiments,[34] or any of "the secrets of the heart."[35]

**5** Knowing, then, that "God is not mocked,"[36] we ought to live worthily of his commandment and glory.

Likewise the deacons should be blameless[37] before his righteousness, as servants of God and Christ and not of men; not slanderers, or double-tongued, not lovers of money, temperate in all matters, compassionate, careful, living according to the truth of the Lord, who became "a servant of all"[38] – to whom, if we are pleasing in the present age, we shall also obtain the age to come, inasmuch as he promised to raise us from the dead. And if we bear our citizenship worthy of him,[39] then "we shall also reign with him"[40] – provided, of course, that we have faith.

Similarly also the younger ones must be blameless in all things, especially taking thought of purity and bridling themselves

---

[30] 1 Clement ch. 1.

[31] 1 Clement ch. 21.

[32] 1 Timothy 5:5; *cf.* 1 Thessalonians 5: 17.

[33] 1 Clement ch. 41.

[34] 1 Clement ch. 21.

[35] 1 Corinthians 14:25.

[36] Galatians 6:7.

[37] *Cf.* 1 Timothy 3:8–13.

[38] Mark 9:35. There is a play here on the word "deacon," which means literally "a servant."

[39] 1 Clement 21; *cf.* Philippians 1:27; Colossians 1:10.

[40] 2 Timothy 2:12; 1 Corinthians 4:8.

from all evil. It is a fine thing to cut oneself off from the lusts that are in the world, for "every passion of the flesh wages war against the Spirit,"[41] and "neither fornicators nor the effeminate nor homosexuals will inherit the Kingdom of God,"[42] nor those who do perverse things. Wherefore it is necessary to refrain from all these things, and be obedient to the presbyters and deacons as unto God and Christ.[43] And the young women must live with blameless and pure conscience.[44]

**6** Also the presbyters must be compassionate, merciful to all, turning back those who have gone astray, looking after the sick,[45] not neglecting widow[46] or orphan or one that is poor; but "always taking thought for what is honorable in the sight of God and of men,"[47] refraining from all anger, partiality, unjust judgment, keeping far from all love of money, not hastily believing evil of anyone, nor being severe in judgment,[48] knowing that we all owe the debt of sin. If, then, we pray the Lord to forgive us, we ourselves ought also to forgive[49]; for we are before the eyes of the Lord and God, and "everyone shall stand before the judgment seat of Christ and each of us shall give an account of himself."[50] So then let us "serve him with fear and all reverence,"[51] as he himself has commanded, and also the apostles who preached the Gospel to us and the prophets who foretold[52] the coming of the Lord. Let

---

[41] 1 Peter 2:11; Galatians 5:17.

[42] 1 Corinthians 6:9, 10.

[43] *Cf.* Magnesians, ch. 2, 6, 13; Trallians, ch. 2, 3; Smyrnaeans, ch. 8; Polycarp, ch. 6.

[44] 1 Clement, ch. 1.

[45] 1 Clement, ch. 59.

[46] *Cf.* Polycarp, ch. 4; Smyrnaeans, ch. 6.

[47] 2 Corinthians 8:21; Romams 12:27; Proverbs 3:4.

[48] *Cf.* 1 Timothy 5:19ff.

[49] Matthew 6:12, 14, 15.

[50] Romans 14:10, 12; *cf.* 2 Corinthians 5:10.

[51] *Cf.* ch. 2; Psalm 2:11; Hebrews 12:28.

[52] Acts 7:52; 1 Clement, ch. 17.

us be zealous for that which is good, refraining from occasions of scandal and from false brethren, and those who bear in hypocrisy the name of the Lord, who deceive empty-headed people.

7 For "whosoever does not confess that Jesus Christ has come in the flesh is antichrist"[53];and whosoever does not confess the testimony of the cross "is of the devil"[54]; and whosoever perverts the sayings of the Lord[55] to suit his own lusts and says there is neither resurrection nor judgment – such a one is the first-born of Satan.[56] Let us, therefore, forsake the vanity of the crowd and their false teachings[57] and turn back to the word delivered to us from the beginning, "watching unto prayer"[58] and continuing steadfast in fasting, beseeching fervently the all-seeing God[59] "to lead us not into temptation,"[60] even as the Lord said, "The spirit indeed is willing, but the flesh is weak."[61]

**8** Let us, then, hold steadfastly and unceasingly to our Hope[62] and to the Pledge[63] of our righteousness, that is, Christ Jesus, "who bore our sins in his own body on the tree, who committed no sin, neither was guile found on his lips"[64];but for our sakes he endured everything that we might live in him. Therefore let us be imitators of his patient endurance, and if we suffer for the sake of his name,

---

[53] 1 John 4:2, 3; 2:22; 2 John 7.

[54] 1 John 3:8.

[55] *Cf.* 1 Clement, ch. 53.

[56] See Irenaeus, *Adv. haer.* III. 3:4; Eusebius, *Hist. eccl.*, IV, ch. 14; and Martyrdom of Polycarp, Epilogue.

[57] *Cf.* ch. 2; 1 Clement, ch. 7, 9.

[58] 1 Peter 4:7.

[59] 1 Clement, ch. 55, 64.

[60] Matthew 6:13.

[61] Matthew 26:41; *cf.* Mark 14:38.

[62] Colossians 1:27; 1 Timothy 1:1; Magnesians, ch. 11; Trallians, ch. 2.

[63] Ephesians 1:14; 2 Corinthians 1:22; 5:5.

[64] 1 Peter 2:24, 22.

let us glorify him.[65] For he set us this example[66] in his own Person, and this is what we believed.

**9** Now I exhort all of you to be obedient to the word of righteousness[67] and to exercise all patient endurance, such as you have seen with your very eyes, not only in the blessed Ignatius and Zosimus and Rufus, but also in others who were of your membership, and in Paul himself and the rest of the apostles; being persuaded that all these "did not run in vain,"[68] but in faith and righteousness, and that they are now in their deserved place[69] with the Lord, in whose suffering they also shared. For they "loved not this present world,"[70] but Him who died on our behalf and was raised by God for our sakes.[71]

**10** Stand[72] firm, therefore, in these things and follow the example of the Lord, "steadfast and immovable"[73] in the faith, "loving the brotherhood,"[74] "cherishing one another,"[75] "fellow companions in the truth"[76]; in "the gentleness of the Lord preferring one another"[77] and despising no one. "Whenever you are able to do a kindness, do not put it off,"[78] because "almsgiving frees from death."[79] All of you submit yourselves to one another,[80]

---

[65] 1 Peter 4:15, 16.

[66] 1 Peter 2:21; 1 Clement, ch. 16.

[67] Hebrews 5:13.

[68] Philippians 2:16; *cf.* Galatians 2:2.

[69] 1 Clement ch. 5.

[70] 2 Timothy 4:10.

[71] 2 Corinthians 5:15; *cf.* 1 Thessalonians 5:10.

[72] With this chapter the original Greek text is no longer extant (except for ch. 13). The translation is from the Latin.

[73] 1 Corinthians 15:58; Colossians 1:23.

[74] 1 Peter 2:17.

[75] 1 Peter 3:8; Romans 12:10.

[76] 3 John 8.

[77] 2 Corinthians 10:1; Romans 12:10.

[78] Proverbs 3:28.

[79] Tobit 4:10.

[80] 1 Peter 5:5.

having your manner of life above reproach from the heathen, so that you may receive praise for your good works and the Lord may not be blasphemed on your account.[81] "Woe to them, however, through whom the name of the Lord is blasphemed."[82] Therefore, all of you teach the sobriety in which you are yourselves living.

**11** I have been exceedingly grieved on account of Valens, who was formerly a presbyter among you, because he so forgot the office that was given him. I warn you, therefore, to refrain from the love of money and be pure and truthful. "Shun evil of every kind."[83] For how shall he who cannot govern himself in these things teach another?[84] If anyone does not refrain from the love of money he will be defiled by idolatry[85] and so be judged as if he were one of the heathen, "who are ignorant of the judgment of the Lord."[86] Or "do we not know that the saints will judge the world," as Paul teaches?[87] However, I have neither observed nor heard of any such thing among you, with whom blessed Paul labored and who were his epistles in the beginning.[88] Of you he boasted in all the churches[89] which at that time alone knew God; for we did not as yet know him. I am, therefore, very grieved indeed for that man and his wife. "May the Lord grant them true repentance."[90] But you, too, must be moderate in this matter; and "do not consider such persons as enemies,"[91] but reclaim them as suffering and

---

[81] 1 Peter 2:12.

[82] Isaiah 52:5; Trallians, ch. 8.

[83] 1 Thessalonians 5:22.

[84] 1 Timothy 3:5.

[85] Colossians 3:5; Ephesians 5:5.

[86] Jeremiah 5:4.

[87] 1 Corinthians 6:2.

[88] Or, "who were mentioned in the beginning of his epistle." Philippians 4:15; *cf.* 2 Corinthians 3:2; 1 Clement ch. 47.

[89] Philippians 2:16; 2 Thessalonians 1:4.

[90] 2 Timothy 2:25; 1:18.

[91] 2 Thessalonians 3:15.

straying members,[92] in order that you may save the whole body of you.[93] For in doing this you will edify yourselves.[94]

**12** I am confident, indeed, that you are well versed in the sacred Scriptures and that nothing escapes you[95] – something not granted to me – only, as it is said in these Scriptures, "be angry but sin not"[96] and "let not the sun go down on your anger."[97] Blessed is he who remembers this. I believe it is so with you. May God and the Father of our Lord Jesus Christ, and the eternal High Priest himself, the Son of God, Jesus Christ, build you up in faith and truth and in all gentleness, without anger and in patient endurance, in long-suffering, forbearance, and purity; and give you a portion and share[98] among his saints, and to us also along with you, and to all under heaven who are destined to believe[99] in our Lord Jesus Christ and in "his Father who raised him from the dead."[100] "Pray for all the saints."[101] "Pray also for emperors and magistrates and rulers,"[102] and for "those who persecute and hate you,"[103] and for "the enemies of the cross,"[104] that your fruit may be manifest in all,[105] so that you may be perfected in him.[106]

---

[92] 1 Clement, ch. 59.

[93] 1 Clement, ch. 37.

[94] 1 Thessalonians 5:11.

[95] 1 Clement, ch. 53; *cf.* Ignatius to the Ephesians, ch. 14.

[96] Psalm 4:5.

[97] Ephesians 4:26.

[98] Acts 8:21.

[99] Colossians 1:23; *cf.* 1 Timothy 1:16.

[100] Galatians 1:1; Colossians 2:12; 1 Peter 1:21.

[101] Ephesians 6:18.

[102] 1 Timothy 2:1, 2; *cf.* 1 Clement, ch. 61.

[103] Matthew 5:44; Luke 6:27.

[104] Philemon 3:18.

[105] 1 Timothy 4:15.

[106] Colossians 2:10; James 1:4.

**13** Both[107] you and Ignatius have written me that if anyone is leaving for Syria he should take your letter along too. I shall attend to this if I have a favorable opportunity – either myself or one whom I shall send to represent you as well as me. We are sending you the letters of Ignatius, those he addressed to us and any others we had by us, just as you requested. They are herewith appended to this letter. From them you can derive great benefit, for they are concerned with faith and patient endurance and all the edification pertaining to the Lord. Of Ignatius himself and those who are with him, let us have any reliable information that you know.

**14** I am sending you this letter by Crescens, whom I recently commended to you and now commend him again. He has lived with us blamelessly, and I believe he will do so among you.[108] I also commend to you his sister, when she arrives among you. Farewell in the Lord Jesus Christ in grace,[109] both you and all who are yours. Amen.

---

[107] The Greek original of this chapter, except for the last sentence, has been preserved by Eusebius (*Hist. eccl.* IV, 36: 13–15).

[108] *Cf.* 1 Clement 63:3.

[109] Smyrnaeans, ch. 13.

# The Martyrdom of Polycarp

## Introduction

The letter of the Church in Smyrna to the church in Philomelium, commonly known as "The Martyrdom of Polycarp," is the oldest account of the martyrdom of a Christian that has come down to us outside of the pages of the New Testament. It is also our earliest testimony to the veneration of the relics of the saints and the annual liturgical celebration of their day of martyrdom. The arrest and death of Polycarp and other companions are recounted by eyewitnesses.

## The letter of the Church of Smyrna to the Church at Philomelium

The church of God that sojourns at Smyrna to the church of God that sojourns at Philomelium, and to all those of the holy and catholic Church who sojourn in every place: may mercy, peace, and love be multiplied from God the Father and our Lord Jesus Christ.[110]

**1** We write you, brethren, the things concerning those who suffered martyrdom, especially the blessed Polycarp, who put an end to the persecution by sealing it, so to speak, through his own witness. For almost everything that led up to it happened in order that the Lord might show once again a martyrdom conformable to the Gospel.[111] For he waited to be betrayed, just as the Lord did, to the end that we also might be imitators of him, "not looking only to that which concerns ourselves, but also to that which concerns

---

[110] 1 Peter 1:1, 2; Jude 2.

[111] John 18:37; *cf.* Revelation 1:5; 3:14. The Passion of Christ is the pattern of that of his martyrs. *Cf.* Polycarp to the Philippians, ch. 8.

our neighbors."[112] For it is a mark of true and steadfast love for one not only to desire to be saved oneself, but all the brethren also.

**2** Blessed and noble, indeed, are all the martyrdoms that have taken place according to God's will; for we ought to be very reverent in ascribing to God power over all things. For who would not admire their nobility and patient endurance and love of their Master? Some of them, so torn by scourging that the anatomy of their flesh was visible as far as the inner veins and arteries, endured with such patience that even the bystanders took pity and wept; others achieved such heroism that not one of them uttered a cry or a groan, thus showing all of us that at the very hour of their tortures the most noble martyrs of Christ were no longer in the flesh, but rather that the Lord stood by them and conversed with them. And giving themselves over to the grace of Christ they despised the tortures of this world, in the space of one hour purchasing for themselves the life eternal. To them the fire of their inhuman tortures was cold; for they set before their eyes escape from the fire that is everlasting and never quenched,[113] while with the eyes of their heart they gazed upon the good things reserved for those that endure patiently, "which things neither ear has heard nor eye has seen, nor has there entered into the heart of man."[114] But they were shown to them by the Lord, for they were no longer men, but were already angels. Similarly, those condemned to the wild beasts endured fearful punishments, being made to lie on sharp shells and punished with other forms of various torments, in order that the devil might bring them, if possible, by means of the prolonged punishment, to a denial of their faith.

**3** Many, indeed, were the machinations of the devil against them. But, thanks be to God, he did not prevail against them all. For the most noble Germanicus encouraged their timidity through his own patient endurance – who also fought with the beasts in a distinguished way. For when the proconsul, wishing

[112] Philippians 2:4.

[113] Matthew 3:12; Mark 9:43; Ignatius to the Ephesians, ch. 16.

[114] 1 Corinthians 2:9; Isaiah 64:4; 65:16.

to persuade him, bade him have pity on his youth, he forcibly dragged the wild beast toward himself,[115] wishing to obtain more quickly a release from their wicked and lawless life. From this circumstance, all the crowd, marveling at the heroism of the God-loving and God-fearing race of the Christians, shouted: "Away with the atheists![116] Make search for Polycarp!"

**4** But a Phrygian[117] named Quintus, lately arrived from Phrygia, took fright when he saw the wild beasts. In fact, he was the one who had forced himself and some others to come forward voluntarily. The proconsul by much entreaty persuaded him to take the oath and to offer the sacrifice. For this reason, therefore, brethren, we do not praise those who come forward of their own accord, since the Gospel does not teach us so to do.[118]

**5** The most admirable Polycarp, when he first heard of it, was not perturbed, but desired to remain in the city. But the majority induced him to withdraw, so he retired to a farm not far from the city and there stayed with a few friends, doing nothing else night and day but pray for all men and for the churches throughout the world, as was his constant habit.[119] And while he was praying, it so happened, three days before his arrest, that he had a vision and saw his pillow blazing with fire, and turning to those who were with him he said, "I must be burned alive."

**6** And while those who were searching for him continued their quest, he moved to another farm, and forthwith those searching for him arrived. And when they did not find him, they seized two young slaves, one of whom confessed under torture. For it was really impossible to conceal him, since the very ones who betrayed

---

[115] *Cf.* Ignatius to the Romans, ch. 5.

[116] *Cf.* Justin, *Apol.* I, chs. 6; 13; Athenagoras, Leg., chs. 3 ff.

[117] The name "Phrygian" was often given to an adherent of the Montanist sect. See the Introduction.

[118] *Cf.* Matt 10:23; John 7:1; 8:59; 10:39; Acts 13:51; 17:14; 19:30, 31.

[119] *Cf.* Polycarp, Phil. 12:3.

him were of his own household.[120] And the chief of the police, who chanced to have the same name as Herod, was zealous to bring him into the arena in order that he might fulfill his own appointed lot of being made a partaker with Christ; while those who betrayed him should suffer the punishment of Judas himself.

**7** Therefore, taking the young slave on Friday about suppertime, the police, mounted and with their customary arms, set out as though "hastening after a robber."[121] And late in the evening they came up with him and found Polycarp in bed in the upper room of a small cottage. Even so he could have escaped to another farm, but he did not wish to do so, saying, "God's will be done."[122] Thus, when he heard of their arrival, he went downstairs and talked with them, while those who looked on marveled at his age and constancy, and at how there should be such zeal over the arrest of so old a man. Straightway he ordered food and drink, as much as they wished, to be set before them at that hour, and he asked them to give him an hour so that he might pray undisturbed. And when they consented, he stood and prayed – being so filled with the grace of God that for two hours he could not hold his peace, to the amazement of those who heard. And many repented that they had come to get such a devout old man.

**8** When at last he had finished his prayer, in which he remembered all who had met with him at any time, both small and great, both those with and those without renown, and the whole catholic Church throughout the world, the hour of departure having come, they mounted him on an ass and brought him into the city. It was a great Sabbath.[123] And there the chief of the police, Herod, and his father, Nicetas, met him and transferred him to their carriage, and tried to persuade him, as they sat beside him,

---

[120] *Cf.* Matt. 10:36.

[121] Matt. 26:55.

[122] Matt. 6:10; Acts 21:14.

[123] *Cf.* John 19:31.

saying, "What harm is there to say, 'Caesar is Lord,' and to offer incense and all that sort of thing, and to save yourself?"

At first he did not answer them.[124] But when they persisted, he said, "I am not going to do what you advise me."

Then when they failed to persuade him, they uttered dire threats and made him get out with such speed that in dismounting from the carriage he bruised his shin. But without turning around, as though nothing had happened, he proceeded swiftly, and was led into the arena, there being such a tumult in the arena that no one could be heard.

**9** But as Polycarp was entering the arena, a voice from heaven[125] came to him, saying, "Be strong, Polycarp, and play the man."[126] No one saw the one speaking, but those of our people who were present heard the voice.[127]

And when finally he was brought up, there was a great tumult on hearing that Polycarp had been arrested. Therefore, when he was brought before him, the proconsul asked him if he were Polycarp. And when he confessed that he was, he tried to persuade him to deny the faith, saying, "Have respect to your age" – and other things that customarily follow this, such as, "Swear by the fortune of Caesar; change your mind; say, 'Away with the atheists!'"

But Polycarp looked with earnest face at the whole crowd of lawless heathen in the arena, and motioned to them with his hand. Then, groaning and looking up to heaven, he said, "Away with the atheists!"

But the proconsul was insistent and said: "Take the oath, and I shall release you. Curse Christ."

---

[124] *Cf.* Mark 14:61; John 19:9, 10.

[125] *Cf.* John 12:28.

[126] Joshua 1:6, 7, 9; *cf.* Deuteronomy 31:7, 23; Psalm 26:15; 30:24.

[127] Acts 9:7.

Polycarp said: "Eighty-six years I have served him, and he never did me any wrong. How can I blaspheme my King who saved me?"

**10** And upon his persisting still and saying, "Swear by the fortune of Caesar," he answered, "If you vainly suppose that I shall swear by the fortune of Caesar, as you say, and pretend that you do not know who I am, listen plainly: I am a Christian. But if you desire to learn the teaching of Christianity, appoint a day and give me a hearing."

The proconsul said, "Try to persuade the people."

But Polycarp said, "You, I should deem worthy of an account; for we have been taught to render honor, as is befitting, to rulers and authorities appointed by God[128] so far as it does us no harm; but as for these, I do not consider them worthy that I should make defense to them."

**11** But the proconsul said: "I have wild beasts. I shall throw you to them, if you do not change your mind."

But he said: "Call them. For repentance from the better to the worse is not permitted us; but it is noble to change from what is evil to what is righteous."

And again he said to him, "I shall have you consumed with fire, if you despise the wild beasts, unless you change your mind."

But Polycarp said: "The fire you threaten burns but an hour and is quenched after a little; for you do not know the fire of the coming judgment and everlasting punishment that is laid up for the impious. But why do you delay? Come, do what you will."

**12** And when he had said these things and many more besides he was inspired with courage and joy, and his face was full of grace, so that not only did it not fall with dismay at the things said to him, but on the contrary, the proconsul was astonished, and sent his own herald into the midst of the arena to proclaim three times: "Polycarp has confessed himself to be a Christian."

---

[128] Romans 13:1, 7; 1 Peter 2:13 ff.; 1 Clement, ch. 61.

When this was said by the herald, the entire crowd of heathen and Jews who lived in Smyrna[129] shouted with uncontrollable anger and a great cry: "This one is the teacher of Asia, the father of the Christians, the destroyer of our gods, who teaches many not to sacrifice nor to worship."[130]

Such things they shouted and asked the Asiarch Philip[131] that he let loose a lion on Polycarp. But he said it was not possible for him to do so, since he had brought the wild-beast sports to a close. Then they decided to shout with one accord that he burn Polycarp alive. For it was necessary that the vision which had appeared to him about his pillow should be fulfilled, when he saw it burning while he was praying, and turning around had said prophetically to the faithful who were with him, "I must be burned alive."[132]

**13** Then these things happened with such dispatch, quicker than can be told – the crowds in so great a hurry to gather wood and kindling from the workshops and the baths, the Jews being especially zealous, as usual, to assist with this. When the fire was ready, and he had divested himself of all his clothes and unfastened his belt, he tried to take off his shoes, though he was not heretofore in the habit of doing this because each of the faithful always vied with one another as to which of them would be first to touch his body. For he had always been honored, even before his martyrdom, for his holy life. Straightway then, they set about him the material prepared for the pyre. And when they were about to nail him also, he said: "Leave me as I am. For he who grants me to endure the fire will enable me also to remain on the pyre unmoved, without the security you desire from the nails."

**14** So they did not nail him, but tied him. And with his hands put behind him and tied, like a noble ram out of a great flock

---

[129] *Cf.* Revelation 2:9.

[130] *Cf.* Acts 16:20, 21.

[131] The Asiarchs were officials who maintained the cult of Rome and the emperor in the province of Asia. *Cf.* Acts 19:31.

[132] *Cf.* ch. 5.

ready for sacrifice, a burnt offering ready and acceptable to God, he looked up to heaven and said:

"O Lord God Almighty,[133] Father of thy beloved and blessed Servant Jesus Christ, through whom we have received full knowledge of thee, the God of angels and powers and of all creation[134], and of the whole race of the righteous who live before thee, I thank thee that thou hast counted me, worthy of this day and this hour[135], that I should have a part in the number of thy martyrs, in the cup of thy Christ[136], to the resurrection of eternal life, both of soul and body[137], in the immortality of the Holy Spirit. Among them may I be received in thy presence this day as a rich and acceptable sacrifice, just as thou hast prepared and revealed beforehand and fulfilled, thou that art the true God without any falsehood. For this and for everything I praise thee, I bless thee, I glorify thee, through the eternal and heavenly High Priest, Jesus Christ, thy beloved Servant, through whom be glory to thee with him and Holy Spirit both now and unto the ages to come. Amen."

**15** And when he had concluded the Amen and finished his prayer, the men attending to the fire lighted it. And when the flame flashed forth, we saw a miracle, we to whom it was given to see. And we are preserved in order to relate to the rest what happened. For the fire made the shape of a vaulted chamber, like a ship's sail filled by the wind, and made a wall around the body of the martyr. And he was in the midst, not as burning flesh, but as bread baking or as gold and silver refined in a furnace. And we perceived such a sweet aroma as the breath of incense or some other precious spice.

**16** At length, when the lawless men saw that his body could not be consumed by the fire, they commanded an executioner to

---

[133] Revelation 4:8; 11:17; 15:3; 16:7; 21:22.

[134] Psalm 58:6; Judith 9:12, 14.

[135] *Cf.* John 12:27.

[136] *Cf.* Mark 10:38, 39; Matthew 20:22, 23; 26:39.

[137] *Cf.* John 5:29.

go to him and stab him with a dagger. And when he did this [a dove and][138] a great quantity of blood came forth, so that the fire was quenched and the whole crowd marveled that there should be such a difference between the unbelievers and the elect. And certainly the most admirable Polycarp was one of these elect, in whose times among us he showed himself an apostolic and prophetic teacher and bishop of the catholic Church in Smyrna.[139] Indeed, every utterance that came from his mouth was accomplished and will be accomplished.

**17** But the jealous and malicious evil one, the adversary of the race of the righteous, seeing the greatness of his martyrdom and his blameless life from the beginning, and how Polycarp was crowned with the wreath of immortality and had borne away an incontestable reward, so contrived it that his corpse should not be taken away by us, although many desired to do this and to have fellowship with his holy flesh. He instigated Nicetas, the father of Herod and brother of Alce,[140] to plead with the magistrate not to give up his body, "else," said he, "they will abandon the Crucified and begin worshiping this one." This was done at the instigation and insistence of the Jews, who also watched when we were going to take him from the fire, being ignorant that we can never forsake Christ, who suffered for the salvation of the whole world of those who are saved, the faultless for the sinners,[141] nor can we ever worship any other. For we worship this One as Son of God, but we love the martyrs as disciples and imitators of the Lord, deservedly so, because of their unsurpassable devotion to their own King and Teacher. May it be also our lot to be their companions and fellow disciples!

**18** The centurion then, seeing the strife excited by the Jews, placed the body in the midst of the fire and burned it. So we later

---

[138] This is considered a late interpolation in the text.

[139] *Cf.* Smyrnaeans 8:2.

[140] *Cf.* the Alce mentioned in Smyrnaeans, ch. 13; Polycarp, ch. 8.

[141] *Cf.* 1 Peter 3:18.

took up his bones, more precious than costly stones and more valuable than gold, and laid them away in a fitting place. There the Lord will permit us, so far as possible, to gather together in joy and gladness to celebrate the day of his martyrdom as a birthday, in memory of those athletes who have gone before, and to train and make ready those who are to come hereafter.

**19** Such are the things concerning the blessed Polycarp, who, martyred at Smyrna along with twelve others from Philadelphia, is alone remembered so much the more by everyone, that he is even spoken of by the heathen in every place. He was not only a noble teacher, but also a distinguished martyr, whose martyrdom all desire to imitate as one according to the Gospel of Christ. By his patient endurance he overcame the wicked magistrate and so received the crown of immortality; and he rejoices with the apostles and all the righteous to glorify God the Father Almighty and to bless our Lord Jesus Christ, the Savior of our souls and Helmsman of our bodies and Shepherd[142] of the catholic Church throughout the world.

**20** You requested, indeed, that these things be related to you more fully, but for the present we have briefly reported them through our brother Marcion. When you have informed yourselves of these things, send this letter to the brethren elsewhere, in order that they too might glorify the Lord, who makes his choices from his own servants. To him who is able[143] by his grace and bounty to bring us to his everlasting Kingdom, through his Servant, the only-begotten Jesus Christ, be glory, honor, might, majesty, throughout the ages. Greet all the saints. Those with us greet you and also Evarestus, who wrote this, with his whole household.

**21** The blessed Polycarp was martyred on the second day of the first part of the month Xanthicus, the seventh day before the kalends of March, a great Sabbath, at two o'clock P.M.[144] He was

---

[142] 1 Peter 2:25.

[143] *Cf.* Jude 24, 25; 1 Clement, ch. 64.

[144] In the year 156 (a leap year) the Sabbath of Purim was on February 22.

arrested by Herod, when Philip of Tralles was high priest,[145] and Statius Quadratus was proconsul,[146] but in the everlasting reign of our Lord Jesus Christ. To him be glory, honor, majesty, and the eternal throne, from generation to generation. Amen.

**22** We bid you farewell, brethren, as you live by the word of Jesus Christ according to the Gospel, with whom be glory to God the Father and Holy Spirit, unto the salvation of his holy elect; just as the blessed Polycarp suffered martyrdom, in whose footsteps may it be our lot to be found in the Kingdom of Jesus Christ.

These things Gaius[147] copied from the papers of Irenaeus, a disciple of Polycarp; he also lived with Irenaeus. And Isocrates, wrote it in Corinth from the copy of Gaius. Grace be with all.

I, Pionius, again wrote it from the aforementioned copy, having searched for it according to a revelation of the blessed Polycarp, who appeared to me, as I shall explain in the sequel. I gathered it together when it was almost worn out with age, in order that the Lord Jesus Christ might bring me also with his elect unto his heavenly Kingdom. To him be glory with the Father and Holy Spirit unto the ages of ages. Amen.

### *Another Epilogue from the Moscow Manuscript*

**23** These things Gaius copied from the papers of Irenaeus. He also lived with Irenaeus, who had been a disciple of the holy Polycarp. For this Irenaeus, at the time of the martyrdom of Bishop Polycarp, was in Rome and taught many; and many of his excellent and orthodox writings are in circulation, in which he mentions Polycarp, for he was taught by him.[148] He ably refuted every heresy and handed down the ecclesiastical and catholic rule,

---

145 Gaius Julius Philippus was appointed high priest and Asiarch sometime between 149 and 153. The term of office was four years.

146 Lucius Statius Quadratus was consul in 142, but the date when he became proconsul of Asia is unknown. It could have been c. 154–156.

147 This may be the Gaius in Eusebius, *Hist. eccl.* II 25:6.

148 See Irenaeus' Letter to Florinus in Eusebius, *Hist. eccl.* V. 20:6.

as he had received it from the saint. He says this also: that once when Marcion, after whom the Marcionites are called, met the holy Polycarp and said, "Do you know us, Polycarp?" he said to Marcion, "I know you; I know the first-born of Satan."[149] And this fact is also found in the writings of Irenaeus, that on the day and at the hour when Polycarp was martyred in Smyrna, Irenaeus, being in the city of Rome, heard a voice like a trumpet saying, "Polycarp has suffered martyrdom."

From these papers of Irenaeus, then, as was said above, Gaius made a copy, and from Gaius' copy Isocrates made another in Corinth. And I, Pionius, again from the copies of Isocrates wrote according to the revelation of holy Polycarp, when I searched for it, and gathered it together when it was almost worn out with age, in order that the Lord Jesus Christ might bring me with his elect unto his heavenly Kingdom. To whom be glory with the Father and the Son and the Holy Spirit unto the ages of ages. Amen.

---

[149] Irenaeus, *Adv. haer.* III. 3:4.; cf: Polycarp, Phil. 7:1.

5

# Melito of Sardis

## Introduction

Melito of Sardis (c. AD 100 – c. 180) was bishop of Sardis, near Smyrna in Asia Minor. Sardis is one of the cities addressed in the Revelation *(3:1)*.

Eusebius, in his fourth-century *Church History*, quotes a letter of Polycrates, a bishop in Asia Minor, to Bishop Victor of Rome, dated c. AD 186-195. Among other "great lights who have died" in Asia, he names "Melito the eunuch, who governed all things in the Holy Spirit, and who lies at Sardis awaiting the visitation from the heavens when he shall be raised from the dead."[1] Jerome quotes a lost work by Tertullian which recounts that many people considered Melito a prophet.[2]

Melito wrote this homily between AD 160–170. The text reveals that it was a liturgical poem preached during the celebration of the resurrection of Christ. His text is the account of the Passover in the twelfth chapter of Exodus. The form of the homily is based

1 Eusebius, *Hist. eccl.* V. 24.

2 Jerome, *De Viris Illustribus*, ch. 24.

on the Haggadah, the annual retelling of the works of God at Passover.

The Greek title of this text is *Peri Pascha*. The Hebrew word for "to skip" or "to omit" is *Pesach*; in Aramaic and Greek this becomes *Pascha*. This is the word translated "Easter"[3] or "Passover" in English editions of the Bible, referring to God's passing over the homes of the Hebrews when judging the Egyptians. To the Greeks this word has an additional implication, as it resembles the Greek verb *paschō*, "to suffer," and so alludes to the passion and resurrection of Christ.

It is interesting that Melito does not quote the New Testament, though he is obviously well-versed in the oral tradition of the Gospel.

## On the Passover

### Introduction (1-10)

**1** First of all, the Scripture about the Hebrew Exodus has been read and the words of the mystery have been explained as to how the sheep was sacrificed and the people were saved.

**2** Therefore, understand this, O beloved: The mystery of the Passover is new and old, eternal and temporal, corruptible and incorruptible, mortal and immortal in this fashion:

**3** It is old insofar as it concerns the law, but new insofar as it concerns the gospel; temporal insofar as it concerns the type, eternal because of grace; corruptible because of the sacrifice of the sheep, incorruptible because of the life of the Lord; mortal because of his burial in the earth, immortal because of his resurrection from the dead.

---

[3] Acts 12:4 KJV.

**4** The law is old, but the gospel is new; the type was for a time, but grace is forever. The sheep was corruptible, but the Lord is incorruptible, who was crushed as a lamb, but who was resurrected as God. For although he was led to sacrifice as a sheep, yet he was not a sheep; and although he was as a lamb without voice, yet indeed he was not a lamb. The one was the model; the other was found to be the finished product.

**5** For God replaced the lamb, and a man the sheep; but in the man was Christ, who contains all things.

**6** Hence, the sacrifice of the sheep, and the sending of the lamb to slaughter, and the writing of the law – each led to and issued in Christ, for whose sake everything happened in the ancient law, and even more so in the new gospel.

**7** For indeed the law issued in the gospel – the old in the new, both coming forth together from Zion and Jerusalem; and the commandment issued in grace, and the type in the finished product, and the lamb in the Son, and the sheep in a man, and the man in God.

**8** For the one who was born as Son, and led to slaughter as a lamb, and sacrificed as a sheep, and buried as a man, rose up from the dead as God, since he is by nature both God and man.

**9** He is everything: in that he judges he is law, in that he teaches he is gospel, in that he saves he is grace, in that he begets he is Father, in that he is begotten he is Son, in that he suffers he is sheep, in that he is buried he is man, in that he comes to life again he is God.

**10** Such is Jesus Christ, to whom be the glory forever. Amen.

## I. The Meaning of the OT Passover (11-71)

### *A. The Biblical Setting – Exodus 12:11-30 (11-15)*

**11** Now comes the mystery of the Passover, even as it stands written in the law, just as it has been read aloud only moments ago. But I will clearly set forth the significance of the words of this

Scripture, showing how God commanded Moses in Egypt, when he had made his decision, to bind Pharaoh under the lash, but to release Israel from the lash through the hand of Moses.

**12** For see to it, he says, that you take a flawless and perfect lamb, and that you sacrifice it in the evening with the sons of Israel, and that you eat it at night, and in haste. You are not to break any of its bones.

**13** You will do it like this, he says: In a single night you will eat it by families and by tribes, your loins girded, and your staves in your hands. For this is the Lord's Passover, an eternal reminder for the sons of Israel.

**14** Then take the blood of the sheep, and anoint the front door of your houses by placing upon the posts of your entrance-way the sign of the blood, in order to ward off the angel. For behold I will strike Egypt, and in a single night she will be made childless from beast to man.

**15** Then, when Moses sacrificed the sheep and completed the mystery at night together with the sons of Israel, he sealed the doors of their houses in order to protect the people and to ward off the angel.

### *B. Egypt's Calamities (16-29)*

**16** But when the sheep was sacrificed, and the Passover consumed, and the mystery completed, and the people made glad, and Israel sealed, then the angel arrived to strike Egypt, who was neither initiated into the mystery, participant of the Passover, sealed by the blood, nor protected by the Spirit, but who was the enemy and the unbeliever.

**17** In a single night the angel struck and made Egypt childless. For when the angel had encompassed Israel, and had seen her sealed with the blood of the sheep, he advanced against Egypt, and by means of grief subdued the stubborn Pharaoh, clothing him, not with a cloak of mourning, nor with a torn mantle, but with all of Egypt, torn, and mourning for her firstborn.

**18** For all Egypt, plunged in troubles and calamities, in tears and lamentations, came to Pharaoh in utter sadness, not in appearance only, but also in soul, having torn not only her garments but her tender breasts as well.

**19** Indeed it was possible to observe an extraordinary sight: in one place people beating their breasts, in another those wailing, and in the middle of them Pharaoh, mourning, sitting in sackcloth and cinders, shrouded in thick darkness as in a funeral garment, girded with all Egypt as with a tunic of grief.

**20** For Egypt clothed Pharaoh as a cloak of wailing. Such was the mantle that had been woven for his royal body. With just such a cloak did the angel of righteousness clothe the self-willed Pharaoh: with bitter mournfulness, and with thick darkness, and with childlessness. For that angel warred against the firstborn of Egypt. Indeed, swift and insatiate was the death of the firstborn.

**21** And an unusual monument of defeat, set up over those who had fallen dead in a moment, could be seen. For the defeat of those who lay dead became the provisions of death.

**22** If you listen to the narration of this extraordinary event you will be astonished. For these things befell the Egyptians: a long night, and darkness which was touchable, and death which touched, and an angel who oppressed, and Hades which devoured their firstborn.

**23** But you must listen to something still more extraordinary and terrifying: in the darkness which could be touched was hidden death which could not be touched. And the ill-starred Egyptians touched the darkness, while death, on the watch, touched the firstborn of the Egyptians as the angel had commanded.

**24** Therefore, if anyone touched the darkness he was led out by death. Indeed one firstborn, touching a dark body with his hand, and utterly frightened in his soul, cried aloud in misery and in terror: What has my right hand laid hold of? At what does my soul tremble? Who cloaks my whole body with darkness? If you are my father, help me; if my mother, feel sympathy for me; if my brother, speak to me; if my friend, sit with me; if my enemy, go away from me since I am a firstborn son!

**25** And before the firstborn was silent, the long silence held him in its power, saying: You are mine, O firstborn! I, the silence of death, am your destiny.

**26** And another firstborn, taking note of the capture of the firstborn, denied his identity, so that he might not die a bitter death: I am not a firstborn son; I was born like a third child. But he who could not be deceived touched that firstborn, and he fell forward in silence. In a single moment the firstborn fruit of the Egyptians was destroyed. The one first conceived, the one first born, the one sought after, the one chosen was dashed to the ground; not only that of men but that of irrational animals as well.

**27** A lowing was heard in the fields of the earth, of cattle bellowing for their nurslings, a cow standing over her calf, and a mare over her colt. And the rest of the cattle, having just given birth to their offspring and swollen with milk, were lamenting bitterly and piteously for their firstborn.

**28** And there was a wailing and lamentation because of the destruction of the men, because of the destruction of the firstborn who were dead. And all Egypt stank, because of the unburied bodies.

**29** Indeed one could see a frightful spectacle: of the Egyptians there were mothers with dishevelled hair, and fathers who had lost their minds, wailing aloud in terrifying fashion in the Egyptian tongue: O wretched persons that we are! We have lost our firstborn in a single moment! And they were striking their breasts with their hands, beating time in hammerlike fashion to the dance for their dead.

### *C. Israel's Safety (30-33)*

**30** Such was the misfortune which encompassed Egypt. In an instant it made her childless. But Israel, all the while, was being protected by the sacrifice of the sheep and truly was being illumined by its blood which was shed; for the death of the sheep was found to be a rampart for the people.

**31** O inexpressible mystery! the sacrifice of the sheep was found to be the salvation of the people, and the death of the sheep became the life of the people. For its blood warded off the angel.

**32** Tell me, O angel: At what were you turned away? At the sacrifice of the sheep, or the life of the Lord? At the death of the sheep, or the type of the Lord? At the blood of the sheep, or the Spirit of the Lord? Clearly, you were turned away

**33** because you saw the mystery of the Lord taking place in the sheep, the life of the Lord in the sacrifice of the sheep, the type of the Lord in the death of the sheep. For this reason you did not strike Israel, but it was Egypt alone that you made childless.

### *D. Model versus Finished Product (34-38)*

**34** What was this extraordinary mystery? It was Egypt struck to destruction but Israel kept for salvation. Listen to the meaning of this mystery:

**35** Beloved, no speech or event takes place without a pattern or design; every event and speech involves a pattern – that which is spoken, a pattern, and that which happens, a prefiguration – in order that as the event is disclosed through the prefiguration, so also the speech may be brought to expression through its outline.

**36** Without the model, no work of art arises. Is not that which is to come into existence seen through the model which typifies it? For this reason a pattern of that which is to be is made either out of wax, or out of clay, or out of wood, in order that by the smallness of the model, destined to be destroyed, might be seen that thing which is to arise from it – higher than it in size, and mightier than it in power, and more beautiful than it in appearance, and more elaborate than it in ornamentation.

**37** So whenever the thing arises for which the model was made, then that which carried the image of that future thing is destroyed as no longer of use, since it has transmitted its resemblance to that which is by nature true. Therefore, that which once was valuable, is now without value because that which is truly valuable has appeared.

**38** For each thing has its own time: there is a distinct time for the type, there is a distinct time for the material, and there is a distinct time for the truth. You construct the model. You want this, because you see in it the image of the future work. You procure the material for the model. You want this, on account of that which is going to arise because of it. You complete the work and cherish it alone, for only in it do you see both type and the truth.

### *E. Relationship Between OT and NT (39-45)*

**39** Therefore, if it was like this with models of perishable objects, so indeed will it also be with those of imperishable objects. If it was like this with earthly things, so indeed also will it be with heavenly things. For even the Lord's salvation and his truth were prefigured in the people, and the teaching of the gospel was proclaimed in advance by the law.

**40** The people, therefore, became the model for the church, and the law a parabolic sketch. But the gospel became the explanation of the law and its fulfillment, while the church became the storehouse of truth.

**41** Therefore, the type had value prior to its realization, and the parable was wonderful prior to its interpretation. This is to say that the people had value before the church came on the scene, and the law was wonderful before the gospel was brought to light.

**42** But when the church came on the scene, and the gospel was set forth, the type lost its value by surrendering its significance to the truth, and the law was fulfilled by surrendering its significance to the gospel. Just as the type lost its significance by surrendering its image to that which is true by nature, and as the parable lost its significance by being illumined through the interpretation,

**43** So indeed also the law was fulfilled when the gospel was brought to light, and the people lost their significance when the church came on the scene, and the type was destroyed when the Lord appeared. Therefore, those things which once had value are today without value, because the things which have true value have appeared.

**44** For at one time the sacrifice to the sheep was valuable, but now it is without value because of the life of the Lord. The death of the sheep once was valuable, but now it is without value because of the salvation of the Lord. The blood of the sheep once was valuable, but now it is without value because of the Spirit of the Lord. The silent lamb once was valuable, but now it has no value because of the blameless Son. The temple here below once was valuable, but now it is without value because of the Christ from above.

**45** The Jerusalem here below once had value, but now it is without value because of the Jerusalem from above. The meager inheritance once had value; now it is without value because of the abundant grace. For not in one place alone, nor yet in narrow confines, has the glory of God been established, but his grace has been poured out upon the uttermost parts of the inhabited world, and there the almighty God has taken up his dwelling place through Jesus Christ, to whom be the glory for ever. Amen.

### *F. Components of the Mystery of the Passover (46-71)*

#### 1. The Passover (46-47a)

**46** Now that you have heard the explanation of the type and of that which corresponds to it, hear also what goes into making up the mystery. What is the Passover? Indeed its name is derived from that event – "to celebrate the Passover" (*to paschein*) is derived from "to suffer" (*tou pathein*). Therefore, learn who the sufferer is and who he is who suffers along with the sufferer.

**47** Why indeed was the Lord present upon the earth? In order that having clothed himself with the one who suffers, he might lift him up to the heights of heaven.

## 2. The Creation and Fall of Man (47b-48)

In the beginning, when God made heaven and earth, and everything in them through his word, he himself formed man from the earth and shared with that form his own breath, he himself placed him in paradise, which was eastward in Eden, and there they lived most luxuriously.

Then by way of command God gave them this law: For your food you may eat from any tree, but you are not to eat from the tree of the one who knows good and evil. For on the day you eat from it, you most certainly will die.[4]

**48** But man, who is by nature capable of receiving good and evil as soil of the earth is capable of receiving seeds from both sides, welcomed the hostile and greedy counselor, and by having touched that tree transgressed the command, and disobeyed God. As a consequence, he was cast out into this world as a condemned man is cast into prison.

## 3. Consequences of the Fall (49-56)

**49** And when he had fathered many children, and had grown very old, and had returned to the earth through having tasted of the tree, an inheritance was left behind by him for his children. Indeed, he left his children an inheritance – not of chastity but of unchastity, not of immortality but of corruptibility, not of honor but of dishonor, not of freedom but of slavery, not of sovereignty but of tyranny, not of life but of death, not of salvation but of destruction.

**50** Extraordinary and terrifying indeed was the destruction of men upon the earth. For the following things happened to them: They were carried off as slaves by sin, the tyrant, and were led away into the regions of desire where they were totally engulfed by insatiable sensual pleasures – by adultery, by unchastity, by debauchery, by inordinate desires, by avarice, by murders,

---

[4] Genesis 2:17.

by bloodshed, by the tyranny of wickedness, by the tyranny of lawlessness.

**51** For even a father of his own accord lifted up a dagger against his son; and a son used his hands against his father; and the impious person smote the breasts that nourished him; and brother murdered brother; and host wronged his guest; and friend assassinated friend; and one man cut the throat of another with his tyrannous right hand.

**52** Therefore all men on the earth became either murderers, or parricides, or killers of their children. And yet a thing still more dreadful and extraordinary was to be found: A mother attacked the flesh which she gave birth to, a mother attacked those whom her breasts had nourished; and she buried in her belly the fruit of her belly. Indeed, the ill-starred mother became a dreadful tomb, when she devoured the child which she bore in her womb.

**53** But in addition to this there were to be found among men many things still more monstrous and terrifying and brutal: father cohabits with his child, and son and with his mother, and brother with sister, and male with male, and each man lusting after the wife of his neighbor.

**54** Because of these things sin exulted, which, because it was death's collaborator, entered first into the souls of men, and prepared as food for him the bodies of the dead. In every soul sin left its mark, and those in whom it placed its mark were destined to die.

**55** Therefore, all flesh fell under the power of sin, and every body under the dominion of death, for every soul was driven out from its house of flesh. Indeed, that which had been taken from the earth was dissolved again into earth, and that which had been given from God was locked up in Hades. And that beautiful ordered arrangement was dissolved, when the beautiful body was separated (from the soul).

**56** Yes, man was divided up into parts by death. Yes, an extraordinary misfortune and captivity enveloped him: he was dragged away captive under the shadow of death, and the image of the Father remained there desolate. For this reason, therefore, the mystery of the Passover has been completed in the body of the Lord.

### 4. Predictions of Christ's Sufferings (57-65)

**57** Indeed, the Lord prearranged his own sufferings in the patriarchs, and in the prophets, and in the whole people of God, giving his sanction to them through the law and the prophets. For that which was to exist in a new and grandiose fashion was pre-planned long in advance, in order that when it should come into existence one might attain to faith, just because it had been predicted long in advance.

**58** So indeed also the suffering of the Lord, predicted long in advance by means of types, but seen today, has brought about faith, just because it has taken place as predicted. And yet men have taken it as something completely new. Well, the truth of the matter is the mystery of the Lord is both old and new – old insofar as it involved the type, but new insofar as it concerns grace. And what is more, if you pay close attention to this type you will see the real thing through its fulfillment.

**59** Accordingly, if you desire to see the mystery of the Lord, pay close attention to Abel who likewise was put to death, to Isaac who likewise was bound hand and foot, to Joseph who likewise was sold, to Moses who likewise was exposed, to David who likewise was hunted down, to the prophets who likewise suffered because they were the Lord's anointed.

**60** Pay close attention also to the one who was sacrificed as a sheep in the land of Egypt, to the one who smote Egypt and who saved Israel by his blood.

**61** For it was through the voice of prophecy that the mystery of the Lord was proclaimed. Moses, indeed, said to his people:

Surely you will see your life suspended before your eyes night and day, but you surely will not believe on your Life.[5]

**62** And David said: Why were the nations haughty and the people concerned about nothing? The kings of the earth presented themselves and the princes assembled themselves together against the Lord and against his anointed.[6]

**63** And Jeremiah: I am as an innocent lamb being led away to be sacrificed. They plotted evil against me and said: Come! let us throw him a tree for his food, and let us exterminate him from the land of the living, so that his name will never be recalled.[7]

**64** And Isaiah: He was led as a sheep to slaughter, and, as a lamb is silent in the presence of the one who shears it, he did not open his mouth. Therefore who will tell his offspring?[8]

**65** And indeed there were many other things proclaimed by numerous prophets concerning the mystery of the Passover, which is Christ, to whom be the glory forever. Amen.

### 5. Deliverance of Mankind through Christ (66-71)

**66** When this one came from heaven to earth for the sake of the one who suffers, and had clothed himself with that very one through the womb of a virgin, and having come forth as man, he accepted the sufferings of the sufferer through his body which was capable of suffering. And he destroyed those human sufferings by his spirit which was incapable of dying. He killed death which had put man to death.

**67** For this one, who was led away as a lamb, and who was sacrificed as a sheep, by himself delivered us from servitude to the world as from the land of Egypt, and released us from bondage to

---

[5] Deuteronomy 28:66.

[6] Psalm 2:1-2. "Anointed" here is Greek *Christos.*

[7] Jeremiah 11:19.

[8] Isaiah 53:7.

the devil as from the hand of Pharaoh, and sealed our souls by his own spirit and the members of our bodies by his own blood.

**68** This is the one who covered death with shame and who plunged the devil into mourning as Moses did Pharaoh. This is the one who smote lawlessness and deprived injustice of its offspring, as Moses deprived Egypt. This is the one who delivered us from slavery into freedom, from darkness into light, from death into life, from tyranny into an eternal kingdom, and who made us a new priesthood, and a special people forever.

**69** This one is the Passover of our salvation. This is the one who patiently endured many things in many people: This is the one who was murdered in Abel, and bound as a sacrifice in Isaac, and exiled in Jacob, and sold in Joseph, and exposed in Moses, and sacrificed in the lamb, and hunted down in David, and dishonored in the prophets.

**70** This is the one who became human in a virgin, who was hanged on the tree, who was buried in the earth, who was resurrected from among the dead, and who raised mankind up out of the grave below to the heights of heaven.

**71** This is the lamb that was slain. This is the lamb that was silent. This is the one who was born of Mary, that beautiful ewe-lamb. This is the one who was taken from the flock, and was dragged to sacrifice, and was killed in the evening, and was buried at night; the one who was not broken while on the tree, who did not see dissolution while in the earth, who rose up from the dead, and who raised up mankind from the grave below.

## II. The Death of Christ and Israel's Sin (72-99)

### *A. Place and Cause of Christ's Death (72-86)*

**72** This one was murdered. And where was he murdered? In the very center of Jerusalem! Why? Because he had healed their lame, and had cleansed their lepers, and had guided their blind with light, and had raised up their dead. For this reason he suffered. Somewhere it has been written in the law and prophets:

"They paid me back evil for good, and my soul with barrenness[9], plotting evil against me[10], saying, 'Let us bind this just man because he is troublesome to us[11].'"

**73** Why, O Israel did you do this strange injustice? You dishonored the one who had honored you. You held in contempt the one who held you in esteem. You denied the one who publicly acknowledged you. You renounced the one who proclaimed you his own. You killed the one who made you to live. Why did you do this, O Israel?

**74** Has it not been written for your benefit: Do not shed innocent blood lest you die a terrible death[12]? Nevertheless, Israel admits, I killed the Lord! Why? Because it was necessary for him to die. You have deceived yourself, O Israel, rationalizing thus about the death of the Lord.

**75** It was necessary for him to suffer, yes, but not by you; it was necessary for him to be dishonored, but not by you; it was necessary for him to be judged, but not by you; it was necessary for him to be crucified, but not by you, nor by your right hand.

**76** O Israel! You ought to have cried aloud to God with this voice: "O Lord, if it was necessary for your Son to suffer, and if this was your will, let him suffer indeed, but not at my hands. Let him suffer at the hands of strangers. Let him be judged by the uncircumcised. Let him be crucified by the tyrannical right hand, but not by mine."

**77** But you, O Israel, did not cry out to God with this voice, nor did you absolve yourself of guilt before the Lord, nor were you persuaded by his works.

---

9 Psalm 34:14.

10 Psalm 34:4.

11 Isaiah 3:10 LXX.

12 *Cf.* Deuteronomy 19:10; 27:25.

**78** The withered hand which was restored whole to its body did not persuade you; nor did the eyes of the blind which were opened by his hand; nor did the paralyzed bodies restored to health again through his voice; nor did that most extraordinary miracle persuade you, namely, the dead man raised to life from the tomb where already he had been lying for four days. Indeed, dismissing these things, you, to your detriment, prepared the following for the sacrifice of the Lord at eventide: sharp nails, and false witnesses, and fetters, and scourges,

**79** and vinegar, and gall, and a sword, and affliction, and all as though it were for a blood-stained robber. For you brought to him scourges for his body, and the thorns for his head. And you bound those beautiful hands of his, which had formed you from the earth. And that beautiful mouth of his, which had nourished you with life, you filled with gall. And you killed your Lord at the time of the great feast.

**80** Surely you were filled with gaiety, but he was filled with hunger; you drank wine and ate bread, but he vinegar and gall; you wore a happy smile, but he had a sad countenance; you were full of joy, but he was full of trouble; you sang songs, but he was judged; you issued the command, he was crucified; you danced, he was buried; you lay down on a soft bed, but he in a tomb and coffin.

**81** O lawless Israel, why did you commit this extraordinary crime of casting your Lord into new sufferings – your Master, the one who formed you, the one who made you, the one who honored you, the one who called you Israel?

**82** But you were found not really to be Israel, for you did not see God, you did not recognize the Lord, you did not know, O Israel, that this one was the firstborn of God, the one who was begotten before the morning star, the one who caused the light to shine forth, the one who made bright the day, the one who parted the darkness, the one who established the primordial starting point, the one who suspended the earth, the one who quenched the abyss, the one who stretched out the firmament, the one who formed the universe,

**83** the one who set in motion the stars of heaven, the one who caused those luminaries to shine, the one who made the angels in heaven, the one who established their thrones in that place, the one who by himself fashioned man upon the earth. This was the one who chose you, the one who guided you from Adam to Noah, from Noah to Abraham, from Abraham to Isaac and Jacob and the Twelve Patriarchs.

**84** This was the one who guided you into Egypt, and guarded you, and himself kept you well supplied there. This was the one who lighted your route with a column of fire, and provided shade for you by means of a cloud, the one who divided the Red Sea, and led you across it, and scattered your enemy abroad.

**85** This is the one who provided you with manna from heaven, the one who gave you water to drink from a rock, the one who established your laws in Horeb, the one who gave you an inheritance in the land, the one who sent out his prophets to you, the one who raised up your kings.

**86** This is the one who came to you, the one who healed your suffering ones and who resurrected your dead. This is the one whom you sinned against. This is the one whom you wronged. This is the one whom you killed. This is the one whom you sold for silver, although you asked him for the didrachma.

### *B. Israel Brought to Trial (87-93)*

**87** O ungrateful Israel, come here and be judged before me for your ingratitude. How high a price did you place on being created by him? How high a price did you place on the discovery of your fathers? How high a price did you place on the descent into Egypt, and the provision made for you there through the noble Joseph?

**88** How high a price did you place on the ten plagues? How high a price did you place on the nightly column of fire, and the daily cloud, and the crossing of the Red Sea? How high a price did you place on the gift of manna from heaven, and the gift of water from the rock, and the gift of law in Horeb, and the land as an inheritance, and the benefits accorded you there?

**89** How high a price did you place on your suffering people whom he healed when he was present? Set me a price on the withered hand, which he restored whole to its body.

**90** Put me a price on the men born blind, whom he led into light by his voice. Put me a price on those who lay dead, whom he raised up alive from the tomb. Inestimable are the benefits that come to you from him. But you, shamefully, have paid him back with ingratitude, returning to him evil for good, and affliction for favor and death for life –

**91** a person for whom you should have died. Furthermore, if the king of some nation is captured by an enemy, a war is started because of him, fortifications are shattered because of him, cities are plundered because of him, ransom is sent because of him, ambassadors are commissioned because of him in order that he might be surrendered, so that either he might be returned if living, or that he might be buried if dead.

**92** But you, quite to the contrary, voted against your Lord, whom indeed the nations worshipped, and the uncircumcised admired, and the foreigners glorified, over whom Pilate washed his hands. But as for you – you killed this one at the time of the great feast.

**93** Therefore, the feast of unleavened bread has become bitter to you just as it was written: "You will eat unleavened bread with bitter herbs.[13]" Bitter to you are the nails which you made pointed. Bitter to you is the tongue which you sharpened. Bitter to you are the false witnesses whom you brought forward. Bitter to you are the fetters which you prepared. Bitter to you are the scourges which you wove. Bitter to you is Judas whom you furnished with pay. Bitter to you is Herod whom you followed. Bitter to you

[13] Exodus 12:8.

is Caiaphas whom you obeyed. Bitter to you is the gall which you made ready. Bitter to you is the vinegar which you produced. Bitter to you are the thorns which you plucked. Bitter to you are your hands which you bloodied, when you killed your Lord in the midst of Jerusalem.

### *C. Gentiles Are Witnesses of Israel's Crime (94-98)*

**94** Pay attention, all families of the nations, and observe! An extraordinary murder has taken place in the center of Jerusalem, in the city devoted to God's law, in the city of the Hebrews, in the city of the prophets, in the city thought of as just. And who has been murdered? And who is the murderer? I am ashamed to give the answer, but give it I must. For if this murder had taken place at night, or if he had been slain in a desert place, it would be well to keep silent; but it was in the middle of the main street, even in the center of the city, while all were looking on, that the unjust murder of this just person took place.

**95** And thus he was lifted up upon the tree, and an inscription was affixed identifying the one who had been murdered. Who was he? It is painful to tell, but it is more dreadful not to tell. Therefore, hear and tremble because of him for whom the earth trembled.

**96** The one who hung the earth in space, is himself hanged; the one who fixed the heavens in place, is himself impaled; the one who firmly fixed all things, is himself firmly fixed to the tree. The Lord is insulted, God has been murdered, the King of Israel has been destroyed by the right hand of Israel.

**97** O frightful murder! O unheard of injustice! The Lord is disfigured and he is not deemed worthy of a cloak for his naked body, so that he might not be seen exposed. For this reason the stars turned and fled, and the day grew quite dark, in order to hide the naked person hanging on the tree, darkening not the body of the Lord, but the eyes of men.

**98** Yes, even though the people did not tremble, the earth trembled instead; although the people were not afraid, the heavens grew frightened; although the people did not tear their garments, the angels tore theirs; although the people did not lament, the Lord thundered from heaven, and the most high uttered his voice.

### *D. Israel Questioned and Sentenced to Death (99)*

**99** Why was it like this, O Israel? You did not tremble for the Lord. You did not fear for the Lord. You did not lament for the Lord, yet you lamented for your firstborn. You did not tear your garments at the crucifixion of the Lord, yet you tore your garments for your own who were murdered. You forsook the Lord; you were not found by him. You dashed the Lord to the ground; you, too, were dashed to the ground, and lie quite dead.

## III. The Final Triumph of Christ (100-105)

**100** But he arose from the dead and mounted up to the heights of heaven. When the Lord had clothed himself with humanity, and had suffered for the sake of the sufferer, and had been bound for the sake of the imprisoned, and had been judged for the sake of the condemned, and buried for the sake of the one who was buried,

**101** he rose up from the dead, and cried aloud with this voice: Who is he who contends with me?[14] Let him stand in opposition to me. I set the condemned man free; I gave the dead man life; I raised up the one who had been entombed.

**102** Who is my opponent? I, he says, am the Christ. I am the one who destroyed death, and triumphed over the enemy, and trampled Hades under foot, and bound the strong one, and carried off man to the heights of heaven, I, he says, am the Christ.

**103** Therefore, come, all families of men, you who have been befouled with sins, and receive forgiveness for your sins. I am your forgiveness, I am the Passover of your salvation, I am the

---

[14] Isaiah 50:8.

lamb which was sacrificed for you, I am your ransom, I am your light, I am your saviour, I am your resurrection, I am your king, I am leading you up to the heights of heaven, I will show you the eternal Father, I will raise you up by my right hand.

**104** This is the one who made the heavens and the earth, and who in the beginning created man, who was proclaimed through the law and prophets, who became human via the virgin, who was hanged upon a tree, who was buried in the earth, who was resurrected from the dead, and who ascended to the heights of heaven, who sits at the right hand of the Father, who has authority to judge and to save everything, through whom the Father created everything from the beginning of the world to the end of the age.

**105** This is the alpha and the omega. This is the beginning and the end – an indescribable beginning and an incomprehensible end. This is the Christ. This is the king. This is Jesus. This is the general. This is the Lord. This is the one who rose up from the dead. This is the one who sits at the right hand of the Father. He bears the Father and is borne by the Father, to whom be the glory and the power forever. Amen.

The *Peri Pascha* of Melito. Peace to the one who wrote, and to the one who reads, and to those who love the Lord in simplicity of heart.

6

# Athanasius of Alexandria

## Introduction

Born in Alexandria, Egypt, about AD 296, Athanasius received a classical education. He wrote *On the Incarnation* prior to his ordination to the diaconate in AD 319. As secretary to Bishop Alexander of Alexandria, he attended the First Ecumenical Council in Nicaea in AD 325, where the Nicene Creed was formulated.

In AD 328, he was appointed Bishop of Alexandria and served in that role for forty-five years, but his defense of the Nicene Creed against Arianism led to conflicts. Athanasius was exiled five times for his committed defense of the Nicene Creed and the coequality of the Father and the Son, spending a total of seventeen years in exile.

Athanasius' *Life of Saint Anthony* had a profound influence on the growing monastic movement in Gaul and Ireland, serving as a foundational text that shaped the practices, ideals, and structures of monastic life in western Europe.

Despite facing opposition and exile, Athanasius remained steadfast in his beliefs and continued to defend the Church's teachings until his death in AD 373.

## On the Incarnation of the Word

**1** In our last book[1], we dealt fully enough with a few points about the error of the nations regarding the worship of idols, and how those false fears originally arose. And by God's grace, we briefly pointed out that the Word of the Father is Himself divine, and his providence and power in all things, that it is through him that the Father gives order to creation. By him all things live and move and have their being.[2]

Now, Macarius[3], true lover of Christ, let us take a step further in the faith of our religion, and consider also how the Word became Man and was divinely manifest in our midst.

The Jews slander that mystery and the Greeks mock it, but we venerate it. So that, even more because of his apparent degradation, you may have an even greater and fuller piety towards him. For it is a fact that the more unbelievers pour scorn on Him, so much the more does He make His Godhead evident. The things which they, as men, rule out as impossible, he plainly shows to be possible; and what they deride as unworthy, His goodness makes most fitting; and things which these wise men laugh at as merely human, by his own power he shows these to be divine. Thus by what looks like utter poverty and weakness on the cross, he overturns the pretense and parade of the idols, and quietly and hiddenly wins over the mockers and unbelievers to recognize him as God.

In dealing with these matters it is necessary first to recall what has already been said. You must understand why it is that the Word of the Father, so great and so high, has been made manifest in bodily form. He has not assumed a body as if it were proper to his own nature, Rather, being by nature bodiless and existing as

1 Athanasius's treatise *Against the Heathen.*

2 Acts 17:28.

3 Greek *makarios* means "blessed," so Athanasius may have been writing to a man named Macarius or he may simply have meant, "O blessed one."

the Word, by the love for humankind and goodness of his own Father he appeared to us in a human body for our salvation.

So we will begin with the creation of the world and with God its Creator, for the first fact that you must grasp is this: The renewal of creation has been brought about by the Word who made it in the beginning. There is no contradiction if the Father accomplishes its salvation in the same One by whom he created it.

**2** There have been various opinions about the making of the universe and the creation of all things, and each person has proposed the theory that suited his own taste. Some say that all things have come into being spontaneously and as by chance, such as the Epicureans, who deny that there is any Mind behind the universe at all. This view is contrary to all the facts of experience, including their own existence. For if all things had come into being spontaneously, as they claim, then all things would necessarily have simply come into being and be identical and without difference. In the universe everything would be sun or moon or whatever it was, and in the human body the whole would be a hand or eye or foot. But in fact the sun and the moon and the earth are all different things, and even within the human body there are different members, such as the foot and the hand and the head. This distinctness of things indicates, not a spontaneous generation, but a Cause that preceded them; and from that Cause we can apprehend God, the Designer and Maker of all.

Others take the view expressed by Plato, that giant among the Greeks. He said that God made all things out of uncreated matter that already existed, just as the carpenter makes things only out of wood that already exists. They do not realize that saying such things is to implies that God is weak; just as it is surely a weakness of the carpenter that he cannot make anything unless he has the wood. How could God be called Maker and Creator if his ability to make depended on some other cause, namely on matter itself? If God only worked on existing matter and did not himself bring matter into being, then he would be not the Creator but only a craftsman.

There is also the theory of the Gnostics, who have invented for themselves an artificer of all things other than the Father of our Lord Jesus Christ. These people are deeply blinded in what they say. For the Lord said to the Jews, "Have you not read that he who made them from the beginning made them male and female, and said, 'For this reason a man shall leave his father and mother and will cleave to his wife, and the two will be one flesh.'" Then, referring to the Creator, he says, "What God has put together, let not man put asunder"[4]. How can they get a creation independent of the Father out of that? And, again, Saint John makes no exception but says, "All things were made through him, and without him nothing was made."[5] So how could there be another creator besides the Father of Christ?

**3** Such are the notions which men put forward. But the inspired teaching and faith according to Christ casts out their vain talk as godlessness. From it we know that, because there is Mind behind the universe, it did not originate itself; because God is infinite, not finite, creation was not made from pre-existent matter, but out of absolute and utter nothing, and out of non-existence, God brought it into being through the Word.

He says as much in Genesis: "In the beginning God created the heavens and the earth,"[6] and again through that most helpful book The Shepherd, "First of all, believe that there is one God who created and finished all things, and made all things out of nothing."[7] Paul also indicates the same thing when he says, "By faith we understand that the worlds were framed by the word of God, so that the things which are seen were not made of things which are visible."[8]

---

4 Matthew 19:4-6.

5 John 1:3.

6 Genesis 1:1.

7 Shepherd of Hermas 2:1.

8 Hebrews 11:3.

For God is good, or rather, he is the fountainhead of all goodness, and one who is good grudges nothing, so that grudging nothing its existence, he made all things through his own Word, our Lord Jesus Christ. Among all these his earthly creatures he had mercy especially on the human race.

And seeing that, because of the way humanity came into being, it could not endure eternally, he granted a grace which other creatures lacked: He made man in his own image, giving them a share in the power of his own Word; so that, reflecting him and expressing the Mind of God even as he does, they might be able to abide in blessedness, living the true life which is really that of the holy ones in paradise.

But since the will of man could turn either way, God secured this grace that he had given by making it conditional from the first upon two things – namely, a law and a place. He brought them into his own paradise, and gave them a law. If they guarded the grace and retained the loveliness of their original innocence, then the life of paradise should be theirs, without sorrow, pain or care, besides having the promise of their incorruptibility in heaven. But if they transgressed and became evil, they would know that they were incurring that corruption in death according to nature, and no longer live in paradise, but thereafter dying outside of it, would remain in death and in corruption.

This is what holy scripture foretells, proclaiming the command of God, "Of every tree of the garden you may freely eat; but of the tree of the knowledge of good and evil you shall not eat, for in the day that you eat of it you shall surely die."[9] This "You shall surely die" – what else might it be except not merely to die, but to remain in the corruption of death?

**4** You may be wondering why we are discussing the origin of men when we set out to talk about the Incarnation of the Word. But this also properly belongs to the aim of our writing.

---

9 Genesis 2:16–18.

For speaking of the manifestation of the Savior to us, it is necessary also to speak of the origin of human beings, so that you may know that it was our own cause that caused the Word to come down, our transgression that called out his love for us, so that the Lord both came to us and appeared among human beings.

It is we who were the purpose of his embodiment, and for our salvation he so loved us as to born and manifested in a human body. For this is how God had made man, and had willed that man should remain in incorruption.

But when humans turned from the contemplation of God to evil of their own devising, they came inevitably under the law of death. Instead of remaining in the state in which God had created them, they were in process of becoming corrupted entirely, and death had them completely under its dominion. For the transgression of the commandment was making them turn back again according to their nature; and as at the beginning they had come into being out of non-existence, so now they were on the way to returning, through corruption, to non-existence again.

Humankind, whose nature once did not exist, had been called into being by the presence and love of the Word. Inevitably, therefore when they lost the knowledge of God, they lost existence with it. For it is God alone who **is**; evil is non-being, the good is being, since it has come into being from the existing God.

By nature, of course, man is mortal, since he was made from nothing; but he bears also the likeness of the One Who Is, and if he preserves that likeness through constant contemplation, then his nature is deprived of its power and he remains incorrupt, as Wisdom says: "The keeping of his laws is the assurance of incorruption."[10] And being incorrupt, man would be henceforth as God, as holy scripture says, "I said you are gods, and all of you

[10] Wisdom 6:18.

sons of the Most High; but you die like men and fall like any prince."[11]

**5** God had not only made us out of nothing, but had also granted life according to God, by the grace of the Word. But men, turning from eternal things to things corruptible, by counsel of the devil, had themselves become the cause of corruption in death. For, as we said before, though they were by nature subject to corruption, the grace of their participation in the Word granted them to escape from the natural law, had they remained good.

Because of the Word present in them, even natural corruption did not come near them, just as Wisdom says, "God created man for incorruption, and made him in the image of his own eternity, but through the devil's envy death entered the world."[12]

When this happened, humans began to die, and corruption prevailed among them and held sway over them to an even more than natural degree, because it was the penalty of which God had forewarned them for transgressing the commandment. For even in their transgressions, for, having invented wickedness in the beginning and so involved themselves in death and corruption, they had gone on gradually from bad to worse, not stopping at any one kind of evil, but continually, as with insatiable appetite, devising new kinds of sins.

Adulteries and thefts were everywhere, murder and plunder filled the earth, law was disregarded in corruption and injustice, all kinds of iniquities were carried out by all, both individually and jointly. Cities warred against cities, and nations rose up against nations, and the whole earth was torn apart with factions and battles, while each strove to outdo the other in wickedness. Even acts contrary to nature were not far from them, but as the martyr and apostle of Christ says: "Their women exchanged the natural use for what is against nature. Likewise also the men, leaving

---

[11] Psalm 81:6-7.

[12] Wisdom 2:23-24.

natural relations with the woman, were consumed in their lust for one another, men committing shameful acts with men and receiving in themselves the due penalty of their error."[13]

**6** For these reasons, then, because death and corruption were gaining ever firmer hold on them, the human race was perishing. Man, who was created rational[14] and in God's image was disappearing, and the work of God was being undone. For by the law, death, which followed from the transgression, prevailed against us, and from the law there was no escape, for it had been established by God because of the transgression.

The thing that was happening was in truth both monstrous and unfitting. It would, of course, have been unthinkable that God should go back upon His word and that man, having transgressed, should not die; but it was equally monstrous that beings which once had shared the nature of the Word should perish and turn back again into non-existence through corruption.

It was unworthy of the goodness of God that who had been made rational and partakers of the Word should perish, and once again return to non-being through corruption. And it was unworthy of the goodness of God that those created by him should be corrupted through the deceit wrought by the devil upon men; and it was especially improper that the workmanship of God in human beings should be done away, either through their own negligence or through the deceit of the demons.

So, as the rational creatures were being corrupted and such works were perishing, what then was God, being good, to do? Was He to let corruption and death have their way with them? In that case, what was the use of having made them in the beginning? Surely it would have been better never to have been created at all than, having been created, to be neglected and perish; and,

---

[13] Romans 1:26-27

[14] Rational in the original is *logikos*, from the *logos*, meaning word or reason. Athanasius will continue to emphasize this connection between the race of man, created rational in the image of God, and Christ himself, the Word of God.

besides that, such indifference to the ruin of His own work before His very eyes would argue not goodness in God but limitation – and that far more than if He had never created man at all. It was impossible, therefore, that God should leave man to be carried off by corruption, because it would be unfitting and unworthy of the goodness of God.

**7** Yet, while this is true, it is not the whole matter. As we have already noted, it was unthinkable that God, the Father of Truth, should go back upon His word regarding death in order to ensure our continued existence. He could not falsify Himself; what, then, was God to do? Was He to demand repentance from men for their transgression? You might say that that was worthy of God, and argue further that, just as through the transgression they became subject to corruption, so through repentance they might return to incorruption again. But repentance would not guard the consistency of God. For he again would not have remained true if human beings were not held fast by death, for repentance does not recall men from what is natural; all that it does is to make them cease from sinning. If it were only a case of an offence, and not of a subsequent corruption, then repentance would have been well enough; but once transgression had begun, men came under the power of natural corruption, and were deprived of the grace of being in the image of God.

No, repentance could not meet the case. What – or rather Who was needed for such grace and such recalling as we required? Who, but the Word of God himself, who also in the beginning had made all things out of nothing? It was his once more to bring the corruptible to incorruptibility and to maintain for the Father his consistency of character above all. For he alone, being the Word of the Father and above all, was as a result both able to recreate everything, and worthy to suffer on behalf of all and to be an ambassador for all with the Father.

**8** For this purpose, then, the incorporeal and incorruptible and immaterial Word of God entered our world. In one sense, indeed, he was not far from it before, for no part of creation had ever been without him who, while ever abiding in union with the Father, yet fills all things in every place. But now he entered the world in a new way, condescending to us in his love and manifestation to us.

He saw the rational race wasting out of existence, and death reigning over them through corruption. He saw that corruption held us all the closer, because it was the penalty for the transgression. And he saw how unthinkable it would be for the law to be dissolved before it was fulfilled. He saw how unseemly it was that the very things of which he himself was the Creator should be disappearing. And seeing how the surpassing wickedness of men was mounting up against them, he saw also their universal liability to death.

All this He saw and had mercy on our race, moved with compassion for our limitation, unable to endure that death should have the mastery, rather than let his creatures perish and the work of his Father for mankind should be in vain, he took for himself a body, a human body no different from our own. Nor did he will merely to become embodied or merely to appear; had that been so, he could have revealed his divine majesty in some other and better way. No, he took our body – and not only so, but directly from a spotless, stainless virgin, without the agency of human father, a pure body, unmixed from intercourse with man.

The Mighty One, the Creator of all, prepared this body in the virgin as a temple for himself, and made it his own, as the instrument, making himself known and dwelling in it. Thus, taking a body like our own, because all our bodies were liable to the corruption of death, he surrendered his body to death om behalf of all, and offered it to the Father.

This He did out of love for us, so that in his death all might die, and the law of death thereby be undone because – having in his body fulfilled that for which it was appointed – it was thereafter voided of its power against men. He did this so that as human beings had turned towards corruption he might turn them again to incorruptibility and give them life from death by making the body his own, and by the grace of His resurrection banishing death from them as straw from the fire.

**9** The Word perceived that corruption could not be got rid of otherwise than through death; yet he himself, as the Word, being immortal and as the Son of the Father, was not able to die. For this reason, therefore, he assumed a body capable of death, in order that it, through participating in the Word who is above all, might be sufficient for death on behalf of all; and, remaining incorruptible through his indwelling, it might thereafter put an end to corruption for all others as well, by the grace of the resurrection.

It was by surrendering to death the body he had taken, as an offering holy and free from spot, that he immediately abolished death for all who were like him, by offering the like. For since the Word of God was above all, when he offered his own temple and bodily instrument as a substitute for the life of all, he fulfilled in death all that was required. Naturally also, through this union of the immortal Son of God with our human nature, we were all clothed with incorruptibility in the promise of the resurrection.

For the solidarity of mankind is such that, by virtue of the Word's indwelling in a single human body, the corruption which goes with death has lost its power over all. Just as when a great king enters a large city and dwells in one of its houses; because of his dwelling in that single house, the whole city is honored, and enemies and robbers cease to descend on it. Even so is it with the King of all; he has come into our country and dwelt in one body like the others, and so the designs of the enemy against mankind have been foiled, and the corruption of death, which formerly held them in its power, has perished. For the human race would have been utterly dissolved had not the Lord and Savior of all, the Son of God, come among us to put an end to death.

**10** In truth this great work was supremely worthy of the goodness of God. For if a king founded a house or a city, and it is attacked by bandits because of the carelessness of its inhabitants, he in no way abandons it, but avenges it and reclaims it as his own work, having regard not to the people's neglect but rather to his own honor. Much more, then, God the Word of the all-good Father did not neglect the human race that he had created, when it was going to corruption; but rather he blotted out the death which had occurred through the offering of his own body, and corrected their carelessness by his own teaching. In this way he restored the whole nature of man by his own power.

One may be convinced of these things by the theologians of the Savior himself, who have said, "For the love of Christ compels us, because we judge thus: that if One died for all, then all died; and He died for all, that those who live should live no longer for themselves, but for Him who died for them and rose again." from the dead, our Lord Jesus Christ."[15] And again another says: "But we see Jesus, who was made a little lower than the angels, for the suffering of death crowned with glory and honor, that He, by the grace of God, might taste death for everyone."[16] The same writer goes on to point out why it was necessary for none other than God the Word to become incarnate: "For it became Him, for Whom are all things and through Whom are all things, in bringing many sons unto glory, to make the Author of their salvation perfect through suffering."

He means that bringing mankind back from corruption belonged only to him who made them in the beginning. He points out also that the Word assumed a human body, expressly in order that he might offer it in sacrifice for other bodies like his own: "Since then the children are sharers in flesh and blood, He also Himself assumed the same, in order that through death He might bring to nought Him that hath the power of death, that is to say, the Devil, and might rescue those who all their lives were enslaved by the fear of death."

---

15 2 Corinthians 5:14–15

16 Hebrews 2:9.

For by the sacrifice of his own body he did two things: He put an end to the law of death which was against us; and he made a new beginning of life for us, by giving us the hope of resurrection.

For since by man death seized power over men; so by the Word made Man death has been destroyed and life raised up anew. That is what Paul says, that true servant of Christ: "For since by man came death, by man came also the resurrection of the dead. Just as in Adam all die, even so in Christ shall all be made alive," and that which follows.

Now, therefore, when we die, we no longer do so as men condemned to death, but as those who will arise; we await the common resurrection of all, which God, who brought this about and granted it to us, "in his own time will reveal."[17]

This, therefore, is the first cause of the Savior's becoming Man. But there are other reasons that show how wholly fitting is his gracious coming into our midst; and these we must now go on to consider.

**11** When God, who has the power over all things. was making mankind through his own Word, he saw the weakness of their nature, that it was not sufficient of itself to know its Maker, nor to get any idea at all of God. He took pity on them, therefore, and did not leave them destitute of the knowledge of himself, lest their very existence should prove purposeless.

For he is uncreated whereas they had come into being from nothing, and as he is incorporeal whereas human beings had been fashioned here below with a body; and because in every way the things made fell far short of understanding and knowing their Maker, he had mercy on the human race. Because he is good, he did not leave them deprived of the knowledge of himself, lest they should find no profit in existing at all.

For of what use is existence to the ones who were made if they could not know their Maker? How could men be reasonable

---

[17] 1 Timothy 6:15; Titus 1:3.

beings if they had no knowledge of the Word and Reason of the Father, through whom they came to be? Mankind would not have differed at all from the irrational animals if they had knowledge of nothing but earthly things.

And why would God have made them at all if he did not wish to be known by them?

But, in fact, the good God has given them a share in his own Image, that is, in our Lord Jesus Christ, and has made them after the same image and likeness. Why So that, understanding through such grace the image – the Word of the Father – through him they might be able to receive a notion of the Father; and through Him to apprehend the Father; and knowing their Maker they might live the only happy and truly blessed life.

But, as we have already seen, men became foolish, and thought nothing of the grace they had received, and turned away from God. They darkened their own soul so completely that they not only lost the idea of God, but invented for themselves other gods of various kinds. They fashioned idols for themselves in place of the truth, and honored things that are not, rather than God who is, as St. Paul says, "worshipping the creature rather than the Creator."[18]

But worst of all, they transferred the honor which is due to God to wood and stones and to every material object, and even to human beings; and went even further, as we said in our former book. Indeed, they were so darkened that they worshipped demons as gods in fulfilling their own lusts. They sacrificed irrational animals and offered human sacrifices as these gods demanded, and in this way brought themselves more and more under their insane control. Magic arts were taught among them, oracles in various places led men astray, and the cause of everything in human life was traced to the stars as though nothing existed but what can be seen.

---

[18] Romans 1:25.

Impiety and lawlessness were everywhere, and neither God nor his Word were known. Yet he had not hidden himself from the sight of men nor given the knowledge of himself in only one way; but rather he had unfolded it in many forms and by many ways.

**12** The grace of being made in the image of God was sufficient to know the Word, and through him the Father. But as a safeguard against their neglect of this grace, he provided the works of creation so that they might not be ignorant of the Creator.

But since men's carelessness descended gradually to lower and lower things, God made provision by giving them a law, and by sending prophets, men whom they knew. So that if they were not ready to look up to heaven, they might still gain knowledge of their Maker from those close at hand. For men can learn directly about higher things from other men.

Three ways thus lay open to them, by which they might obtain the knowledge of God. They could look up into the immensity of heaven, and by pondering the harmony of creation come to know its Ruler, the Word of the Father, whose providence for all things makes the Father known to all. Or, if they were not ready for this, they could converse with holy men, and through them learn to know God, the Creator of all things, the Father of Christ, and recognize that the worship of idols is godlessness and full of all impiety. Or else, in the third place, they could cease from lawlessness and lead a good life merely by knowing the law. For the law was not given only for the Jews, nor was it solely for their sake that God sent the prophets, though it was to the Jews that they were sent and by the Jews that they were persecuted. The law and the prophets were a sacred school of the knowledge of God and the conduct of the spiritual life for the whole world.

So great, indeed, were the goodness and the love of God. Yet men, bowed down by the pleasures of the moment and by the frauds and illusions of the demons, did not lift up their eyes towards the truth, but sated themselves with evils and sins so that they seemed to be irrational animals, not reasonable men reflecting the likeness of the Word.

**13** What was God to do, then, in face of this dehumanizing of mankind, this universal hiding of the knowledge of himself by the wiles of evil spirits? Keep silence before so great a wrong and let men go on being deceived and kept in ignorance of himself? If so, what was the point of having made them in his own image in the beginning? Then it would have been better for them always to have been brutes, rather than to be made in the image of the Word and then to live like animals.

What was the use of man's ever having had the knowledge of God? Surely it would have been better for God never to have bestowed it, than that men should subsequently be found unworthy to receive it.

And what possible profit could it be to the God who made men, if when made they did not worship him, but regarded others as their makers? He would be found to have made them for others and not for himself. Even an earthly king, though he is only a man, does not allow lands that he possesses to pass into other hands or to go over to other rulers, but he sends letters and friends and even visits them himself to recall them to their allegiance, rather than allow His work to be undone. How much more, then, will God be patient and painstaking with his creatures, that they be not led astray from him to the service of things that do not exist? Especially when such error means for them the cause of their ruin and undoing, and because it is not right that those who had once shared his image should perish.

What then was God to do? What else could he possibly do, being God, but renew his image in mankind, so that through it men might once more come to know him? And how could this be done save by the coming of the very image himself, our Savior Jesus Christ? Men could not have done it, for they are only made "in the image,"[19] nor could angels have done it, for they are not even images of God. The Word of God came himself, because he

[19] Genesis 1:26.

alone, the image of the Father[20], could recreate man made after the image.

But in order to effect this re-creation, first he had to do away with death and corruption. So he rightly assumed a human body, so that in it death might once for all be destroyed, and that men be renewed again according to the image. Only the image of the Father was sufficient for this need.

**14** You know what happens when a portrait that has been painted on a panel becomes obliterated through stains from outside. The artist does not throw away the panel, but the subject of the portrait must come again, and then the likeness is repainted on the same material. Even so the all-holy Son of God, the image of the Father, came and dwelt in our midst, to renew mankind made according to himself, and seek out his lost sheep, even as he says in the Gospel: "I came to seek and to save that which was lost."[21] This also explains his saying to the Jews: "Except a man be born anew…"[22] He was not referring to a man's natural birth from his mother, as they thought, but to the re-birth and re-creation of the soul in the image of God.

But when the madness of idolatry and godlessness filled the world and the knowledge of God was hidden, whose part was it to teach the world about the Father? A man, one might say? But a man cannot traverse the whole world, nor would their words carry sufficient weight if they did; nor were they able by themselves to withstand the deceit and illusion of the demons. For since even the best of men were confused and blinded by the deceit and illusion of demons, how could they convert the souls and minds of others? You cannot put straight in others what is warped in yourself.

But perhaps you will say, then, that creation was enough to teach men about the Father. But if that had been so, such great

---

[20] Colossians 1:15.

[21] Luke 19:10.

[22] John 3:5.

evils would never have occurred. For there was creation already, but it did not prevent men from wallowing in error.

Again, it was God the Word, who sees both soul and mind, who moves everything in creation, who alone could meet the needs of the situation. He alone, whose ordering of the universe reveals the Father, could renew the same teaching.

But how could it be done? Perhaps by the same means as before, through the works of creation. But this was no longer a sure means. Quite the contrary; for men had already missed seeing this before, and had turned their eyes no longer upward but downward.

So, rightly wishing to do good to men, he sojourned here as a man, taking to himself a body like theirs; and through his actions done in that body, on their own level, he taught those who would not learn by other means to know himself, the Word of God, and through him the Father.

**15** He deals with them as a good teacher with his pupils, coming down to their level and using simple means, as Paul says: "Because in the wisdom of God the world in its wisdom knew not God, God thought fit through the simplicity of the news proclaimed to save those who believe."[23]

Men had turned from the contemplation of God above, and were looking for him in the opposite direction, down among created things and things of sense. The Savior of us all, the Word of God, in His great love took to himself a body and moved as Man among men, meeting their senses, so to speak, halfway. He became himself an object for the senses, so that those who were seeking God in sensible things might apprehend the Father through the works which he, the Word of God, did in the body. Human and human-minded as men were, therefore, to whichever side they looked in the sensible world they found themselves taught the truth. Were they awe-struck by creation? They beheld

[23] 1 Corinthians 1:21.

creation confessing Christ as Lord. Did their minds tend to regard men as gods? The uniqueness of the Savior's works marked him, alone of men, as Son of God. Were they drawn to demons? They saw the demons driven out by the Lord and learned that the Word of God alone was God, and that the evil spirits were not gods at all. Were they inclined to hero-worship and the cult of the dead? Then the fact that the Savior had risen from the dead showed them how false these other deities were, and that the Word of the Father is the one true Lord, the Lord even of death.

This is the reason he both born and manifested as Man, for this he died and rose – eclipsing all other human works by his own works and recalling men from all the paths of error to know the Father. As he says himself, "I came to seek and to save that which was lost."[24]

**16** When the minds of men had descended to the level of perceptible things, then the Word submitted to appear in a body, so that, as a Man, he might center their senses on himself, and convince them through his human acts that he is not only a Man but God, the Word and Wisdom of the true God.

This is what Paul tells us when he says: "That ye, being rooted and grounded in love, may be strong to apprehend with all the saints what is the length and breadth and height and depth, and to know the love of God that surpasses knowledge, so that ye may be filled unto all the fullness of God."[25]

For the Word revealed himself everywhere – above, in creation; below, in the incarnation; in the depth, in hades; in the breadth, throughout the world. All things have been filled with the knowledge of God.[26]

For this reason he did not offer the sacrifice on behalf of all immediately when he appeared. For if he had surrendered his

---

[24] Luke 19:10

[25] Ephesians 3:17-19.

[26] *Cf.* Habakkuk 2:14.

body to death and then raised it again at once, we would have seen nothing of him. Instead of that, he stayed in his body and let himself be seen in it, doing acts and giving signs that showed him to be not only a man, but God the Word.

There were thus two things which the Savior did for us by becoming man. He banished death from us and renewed us; and, though he was invisible and imperceptible, he became visible through his works and revealed himself as the Word of the Father, the Ruler and King of the universe.

**17** The Word was not enclosed in his body, nor did his presence in the body prevent his being present elsewhere as well. When he moved his body he did not cease also to direct the universe by his providence. Rather, the marvelous truth is that, being the Word, he was not contained by anything, but rather himself contained all things.

In creation he is present everywhere. He is in essence outside everything but fills all things by his own power, ordering, directing, giving life to all, containing all yet not being contained, being wholly, in every respect, in his Father alone. So also, being in a human body, to which he himself gives life, he is the Source of life to all the universe, present in every part of it, yet outside the whole; and he is revealed both through the works of His body and through his activity in the world.

It is, indeed, the function of soul to behold things that are outside the body through thought, but it cannot affect or move things at a distance. A man cannot transport things from one place to another, for instance, merely by thinking about them; nor can you or I move the sun and the stars just by sitting at home and looking at them.

But for the Word of God in his human nature, it was otherwise. His body was not a limitation for him, but an instrument, so that he was both in it and in all things, and outside all things, resting in the Father alone. And the wonderful thing is that at one and the same time, as Man he was living a human life, and as the Word he was sustaining the life of the universe, and as the Son he was in constant union with the Father.

So that not even his birth from a virgin changed him in any way, nor was he defiled by being in the body – rather, he made the body holy by being in it. For his being in everything does not mean that he shares the nature of everything, only that he gives all things their being and sustains them in it. Just as the sun is not polluted by the contact of its rays with earthly objects, but rather enlightens and purifies them, so much more the all-holy Word of God, the Lord who made the sun, is not polluted by being made known in a body. Rather, the body is cleansed and quickened by the indwelling of the incorruptible One, "Who did no sin, neither was guile found in His mouth."[27]

**18** You must understand, therefore, that when writers on this matter speak of him as eating and drinking and being born, they mean that the body, as a body, was born and sustained with the food proper to its nature; even as God the Word, present in the body yet arranging all things, made known through the works wrought in the body that he was not himself a human being but God the Word. Those acts are rightly said to be His acts, because the body which did them did indeed belong to him and no one else; and it was right for these things to be said of him as a man, to show that his body was a real one and not merely an appearance. From such ordinary acts as being born and taking food, he was recognized as being actually present in the body; but by the extraordinary acts which he did through the body, he proved himself to be the Son of God. This is why he said to the unbelieving Jews: "If I do not the works of My Father, believe Me not; but if I do, even if ye believe not Me, believe My works, that ye may know that the Father is in Me and I in the Father."[28]

Though he is invisible, he is known from the works of creation. So also, when his Godhead is veiled in human nature, His bodily

---

[27] *Cf.* 1 Peter 2:22; Isaiah 53:9.

[28] John 10:37–38.

acts still declare him to be not man only, but the Power and Word of God.

To speak authoritatively to evil spirits, for example, and to drive them out, is not a human act but a divine one; and who could see him curing all the diseases to which mankind is prone, and still think he is human and not God? He cleansed lepers, he made the lame to walk, he opened the ears of the deaf and the eyes of the blind; there was no sickness or weakness that he did not drive away. Even the most casual observer can see that these were acts of God. The healing of the man born blind, for instance: Who but the Father and Maker of man, could thus have restored the faculty denied at birth[29], unless he is himself the Lord of creation?[30]

Therefore, when he came down to us in the beginning, he fashioned for himself a body from the Virgin, in order to provide to all no small proof of his divinity, since he who made the body was the maker of everything else as well. And who, seeing this body coming forth from a Virgin alone without man, would not think that he who is revealed in this body is the Maker and Lord of other bodies also?

Again, consider the miracle at Cana. Would not anyone who saw the substance of water turned into wine understand that he who did it was the Lord and Maker of the water that he changed? It was for the same reason that he walked on the sea as on dry land – to prove to all who saw that he had mastery over all. And the feeding of the multitude, when he made little into much, so that from five loaves five thousand mouths were filled – did that not prove him none other than the very Lord whose providence is over all?

**19** All these things the Savior thought fit to do, so that, recognizing his bodily acts as works of God, men who were blind to his presence in creation might regain knowledge of the Father.

---

[29] Literally, at genesis.

[30] Literally, Lord of genesis.

For, as I said before, who, seeing his authority over demons and their response to it, could doubt that he was, indeed, the Son, the Wisdom and the Power of God?

He made even the creation itself break silence, in that in his death, most wonderfully, before the cross, that monument of victory, all creation confessed with one voice that he who was revealed and suffered in the body was not merely a man but Son of God and Savior of all. The sun veiled its face, the earth quaked, the mountains were rent asunder, all men were struck with awe. These things showed that Christ on the cross was God, and that all creation was his servant and was bearing witness by its fear to its Master's presence. In this way, then, God the Word revealed himself to men through his works.

We must next consider the end of his earthly life and the nature of his bodily death, especially since this is the very center of our faith, and everywhere you hear men speak of it. And by it, too, no less than by his other acts, Christ is revealed as God and Son of God.

**20** We have dealt as far as circumstances and our own understanding permit with the reason for his manifestation in the body. We have seen that to change the corruptible to incorruption was proper to none other than the Savior himself, who in the beginning made all things out of nothing; that only the Image of the Father could re-create the likeness of the Image in men, that none save our Lord Jesus Christ could give immortality to mortals, and that only the Word who orders all things and is alone the Father's true and only-begotten Son could teach men about him and abolish the worship of idols.

But beyond all this, there was a debt owing which needed to be paid; for, as I said before, all men were due to die. Here, then, is the second reason why the Word dwelt among us: So that having proved his divinity by his works, he might offer the sacrifice on behalf of all, surrendering his own temple to death in place of all, to settle man's account with death and free him from the primal transgression. In this act he showed himself mightier than death, displaying his own body as incorruptible, the first-fruits of the resurrection of all.

You must not be surprised if we repeat ourselves in dealing with this subject. We are speaking of the good pleasure of God and of the things which he in his loving wisdom thought fit to do, and it is better to put the same thing in several ways than to run the risk of leaving something out.

Therefore the body of the Word, being a real human body, in spite of its having been uniquely formed from a virgin, was mortal and, like other bodies it was liable to death. Yet by the coming of the Word into it, it was no longer corruptible by its own nature, but because of the indwelling Word of God, corruption could not touch it. Thus it happened that two opposite marvels took place at once: the death of all was consummated in the Lord's body; yet, because the Word was in it, death and corruption were in the same act utterly abolished. Death there had to be, and death for all, so that the due of all might be paid. Therefore, as I said, the Word, since he was immortal, assumed a mortal body so that he might offer it as his own in place of all, and suffering for the sake of all through his union with it, "he might destroy him who has the power of death, that is the devil, and deliver all those who through fear of death were subject to lifelong bondage"[31]

**21** Now that the common Savior of all has died on our behalf, we who believe in Christ no longer die as before, according to the threat of the law. That condemnation has come to an end. But now, corruption has been destroyed by the grace of the resurrection, and henceforth according to the mortality of the body we are dissolved only for the time which God has set for each, "that we may obtain thereby a better resurrection."[32] Like seeds cast into the earth, we do not perish in our dissolution, but like them we shall rise again, death having been destroyed by the grace of the Savior. That is why blessed Paul, who became a guarantor of the resurrection to all,

---

[31] Hebrews 2:14-15.

[32] Hebrews 11:35.

says: "This corruptible must put on incorruption and this mortal must put on immortality; but when this corruptible shall have put on incorruption and this mortal shall have put on immortality, then shall be brought to pass the saying that is written, 'Death is swallowed up in victory. O Death, where is thy sting? O Grave, where is thy victory?'"[33]

"Well then," some people may say, "if the essential thing was that he should surrender his body to death in place of all, why did he not do so as a man privately, instead of going so far as to be crucified? For it would have been more fitting for him to have laid aside his body with honor than to endure such a shameful death. But look at this argument closely, and see how merely human it is, whereas what the Savior did was truly divine and worthy of his divinity for several reasons. First, the death of men under ordinary circumstances is the result of the weakness of their nature. They are essentially impermanent, so after a time they fall ill, and when worn out they die. But the Lord is not weak; he is the Power of God, the Word of God and the very Life himself.

If He had died quietly in his bed like other men it would have looked as if he did so in accordance with nature, and as though he were indeed no more than other men. But because he was himself Word and Life and Power, his body was made strong; and because the death had to be accomplished, he took the occasion to complete the sacrifice, not from himself but from others. For it was not fitting either that the Lord should fall ill, who healed the sicknesses of others; nor again for that body to lose its strength, in which he strengthened to the weaknesses of others also. Here, again, you may say, why then did he not prevent death, as he did sickness? Because it was precisely in order to be able to die that he had taken a body, and to prevent the death would have been to impede the resurrection. And it was equally unfitting for sickness to precede his death, lest it should be thought weakness on the part of him who was in the body. Did he not hunger, then? Yes,

---

33 1 Corinthians 15:53–55.

he hungered, because that was the property of the body, but he did not die of hunger because he whose body hungered was the Lord. Therefore though he died for the ransom of all, "he did not see corruption"[34] but his body rose in perfect soundness, for it belonged to none other than the Life himself.

**22** One might say, that it would have been better for the Lord to have avoided the designs of the Jews against him, to preserve his body from death altogether. But see how unfitting this also would have been for him. For it would not have been fitting for the Word and the Life to inflict death Himself on His own body, so also it was suitable to flee a death inflicted by others. Rather, he pursued it to the uttermost, and in pursuance of his nature neither laid aside his body of his own accord nor escaped the plotting of the Jews. This action showed no limitation or weakness in the Word; for he both waited for death in order to make an end of it, and hastened to complete it for the salvation of all. In addition, since it was not his own death that the Savior came to complete, but that of all mankind, he did not lay aside His body by a death of his own, for he had none, being the Life; but he accepted death at the hands of men, thereby completely to destroy it in his own body.

Again, from the following also one might understand the Lord's body meeting this end. The supreme object of his coming was to bring about the resurrection of the body. The Lord was especially concerned for the resurrection of the body which he was set to accomplish. For he was about to show the incorruption of his own body to all as a monument of victory over death and the blotting out of corruption, a pledge of the future resurrection.

If his body had fallen sick, and the Word had been separated from it in the sight of all, how unbecoming that he who healed the diseases of others should permit his own instrument to waste in illness! How would his miracles of healing be believed, if this were so? People would either laugh at him as unable to drive out disease

[34] *Cf.* Acts 2:31; 13:35; Psalm 15:10.

or else consider him lacking in proper human feeling because he could do so, but did not.

**23** But if, without any illness, he had just concealed his body somewhere privately, "in a corner,"[35] and then suddenly reappeared and said that he had risen from the dead. he would have been regarded merely as a teller of tales; and because there was no witness of his death, nobody would believe his resurrection. Death must precede resurrection, for there could be no resurrection without it. A secret and unwitnessed death would have left the resurrection without any proof or evidence to support it.

Again, since he proclaimed his resurrection openly, why would he die a secret death? Why should he drive out evil spirits in the sight of all, and heal the man blind from birth and change water into wine, in order to convince men that he was the Word, yet not also declare publicly that incorruptibility of his mortal body, so that he might himself be believed to be the Life? And how could his disciples have had boldness in speaking of the resurrection unless they could state it as a fact that he had first died? Or how could their hearers be expected to believe their assertion, unless they themselves also had witnessed his death? For if the Pharisees at the time refused to believe and forced others to deny also, even though the things had happened before their very eyes, then how many excuses for unbelief would they have contrived if it had taken place secretly? How could the end of death and the victory over it be demonstrated, unless the Lord challenged it before the sight of all, proving by the incorruption of his body that henceforward death was null and void?

**24** We must also answer some other questions that might be asked. Some might wonder, even if witnessing a public death was necessary in order that the resurrection may be believed, then he ought to have arranged an honorable death for himself, and avoided the shame of the cross. But even this would have given ground for suspicion that his power over death was limited to the

---

[35] Acts 26:26.

particular kind of death which he chose for himself; and again, that would furnish excuse for disbelieving the resurrection. So, death came to his body not from himself but from enemy action, in order that the Savior might utterly abolish death in whatever form they offered it to him. A noble wrestler, manly and strong, does not choose his antagonists for himself, lest it be thought that he is afraid of some of them. Rather, he lets the spectators choose them, especially if they are hostile, so that he may overthrow anyone they match against him and thus show forth his superior strength.

Even so Christ, the Life of all, our Lord and Savior, did not arrange the manner of his own death lest he should seem to be afraid of some other kind of death, but accepted and endured on the cross a death inflicted by others, specifically by his enemies, a death which to them was supremely terrible and humiliating; and he did this in order that, by destroying even this death, he might himself be believed to be the Life, and the power of death be finally annihilated.

Something marvelous and mighty has thus occurred, for the death which they thought to inflict on him as dishonor and disgrace has become the glorious monument to death's defeat. Therefore he neither endured the death of John, who was beheaded, nor was he sawn asunder, like Isaiah: even in death he preserved his body whole and undivided, so that there should be no excuse for those who would divide the Church.

**25** So much for the objections of those outside the Church. But if anyone from among us, not from love of debate, but from love of learning, wants to know why he suffered death on the cross and not in some other way, we answer that in no other way was it expedient for us, indeed it was good that the Lord endured this for us. He had come to bear the curse that lay on us; and how could he "become a curse"[36] otherwise than by accepting death according to the curse? And that death is the cross, for it is written "Cursed is

[36] Galatians 3:13.

every one that hangs on tree."[37] Again, the death of the Lord is the ransom of all, and by it "the middle wall of partition"[38] is broken down and the calling of the nations comes about. How could he have called us if he had not been crucified? For it is only on the cross that a man dies with arms outstretched. Therefore it was fitting for the Lord to bear this also and to spread out His hands; with the one to draw His ancient people, and with the other those from the nations, and unite both together in himself. For this is what he himself said, indicating the manner of his death,[39] "If I be lifted up, I will draw all men unto Myself."[40]

The devil, the enemy of our race, having fallen from heaven, wanders about our lower atmosphere, and lords it here over his fellow spirits, his equals in disobedience. Through them he not only works illusions in deceived people, but tries to prevent them from ascending upward. About this the apostle says, "According to the prince of the power of the air, of the spirit that now worketh in the sons of disobedience."[41] But the Lord came to overthrow the devil, to purify the air, and to open up for us the way to heaven, as the apostle says, "through the veil, that is to say, His flesh."[42] This had to be done through death, and by what other kind of death could it be done, save by a death in the air, that is, on the cross? for only he that completes his life on the cross dies in the air. So it was fitting that the Lord suffered this death; for being lifted up, He cleansed the air from all the evil influence of the enemy, saying, "I beheld Satan as lightning falling,"[43]and opening the road to heaven, saying again, "Lift up your gates, O ye princes, and be ye lift up, ye everlasting doors."[44] For it was not the Word himself

[37] Deuteronomy 21:23.

[38] Ephesians 2:14.

[39] John 12:33.

[40] John 12:32.

[41] Ephesians 2:2.

[42] Hebrews 10:20.

[43] Luke 10:18.

[44] Psalm 23:7.

who needed the gates opened since he is Lord of all, nor was any of his works closed to their Maker. No, it was we who needed it, we whom he himself carried up in his own body – that body which he first offered to death on behalf of all, and then made through it a path to heaven.

**26** The death on the Cross for our sakes has therefore proved suitable and fitting; and we can see how reasonable it was, and why the salvation of the world could be accomplished in no other way. Even on the cross he did not hide himself from sight; rather, he made all creation witness to the presence of its Maker. Then, having once let it be seen that the temple of his body was truly dead, he did not allow it to remain so for long, but immediately on the third day raised it up, impassable and incorruptible, the pledge and token of his victory over death.

Of course it was within his power to have raised his body and shown it alive immediately after death. But the all-wise Savior did not do this. For some would have denied that it had really or completely died. Besides this, had the interval between his death and resurrection been only two days, the glory of his incorruption might not have appeared. He waited one whole day to show that his body was really dead, and then on the third day showed it to all as incorruptible. The interval was not longer than this, for people might have forgotten about it and grown doubtful whether this were in truth the same body. No, while the affair was still ringing in their ears and their eyes were still straining and their minds in turmoil, and while those who had put him to death were still on the spot and witnessing to the fact of it, the Son of God after three days showed forth the body which had been dead as immortal and incorruptible; and it was evident to all that the body in which the Word dwelt had died, not from any natural weakness, but so that death might be destroyed in it through the power of the Savior.

**27** A very strong proof that death has been destroyed and conquered by the cross is supplied by the fact that all the disciples of Christ disdain death. They take up the offensive against it and, instead of fearing it, they trample on it by the sign of the cross and by faith in Christ, like a dead thing. Before the divine sojourn of the Savior, even the holiest of men were afraid of death, and mourned the dead as those who perish. But now that the Savior has raised his body, death is no longer fearsome, but all those who believe in Christ trample it underfoot as nothing, and would rather die than deny their faith in Christ. For they know well that when they die they do not perish, but truly live become incorruptible through the resurrection. But that devil who formerly exulted wickedly in death, "its pangs having been loosed,"[45] is now the only one who remains truly dead.

There is proof of this, too. For before people believe in Christ, they fear death and are terrified by it; but after they are converted, they disdain death so completely that they go eagerly to meet it, and thereby become witnesses[46] of the Savior's resurrection. Even the young hasten to die, and not only men but women exercise themselves by bodily discipline to meet it. Death has become so weak that even women, who used to be deceived by it, now mock it as dead and paralyzed. Death has become like a tyrant who is completely conquered by a real king, and bound hand and foot. All who pass by laugh him to scorn, buffeting and reviling him, no longer afraid of his cruelty and rage, because of the king who has conquered him. Death has been conquered and exposed by the Savior on the cross. It is bound hand and foot, and all who are in Christ trample it as they pass and deride it, scoffing and saying, "O Death, where is thy victory? O Grave, where is thy sting?"[47]

**28** Is this a weak proof of the weakness of death, do you think? Or is it only a slight indication of the Savior's victory over it, when boys and young girls in Christ look beyond this present life and train themselves to die? Everyone is by nature afraid of death and of bodily dissolution; the most amazing thing is that the one who

---

[45] Acts 2:24.

[46] Or "martyrs" (Greek: *martures*).

[47] 1 Corinthians 15:55.

has put on the faith of the cross scorns this natural fear and is no longer afraid because of the cross.

The natural property of fire is to burn. Suppose that there was a substance such as the Indian asbestos is said to be, which had no fear of being burnt, but rather showed forth the weakness of fire by proving itself unburnable. Then anyone who did not believe the story, if he wished to put it to the test, could put on the fireproof material and touch the fire, thereby being convinced of the weakness of the fire. Or if anyone wanted to see the tyrant bound and helpless, who used to be such a terror to others, he could do so simply by going into the country of the tyrant's conqueror. Even so, if anyone still doubts the conquest of death, even after such great things and after so many have become martyrs in Christ, after the daily scorn shown towards death by his truest servants, he certainly would do well to marvel at so great a thing, but let him not be obstinate in unbelief and shameless in the face of plain facts. Rather, he must be like the man who proves the property of the asbestos, and like him who enters the conqueror's dominions to see the tyrant bound, and he must embrace the faith of Christ, this disbeliever in the conquest of death, and come to his teaching. Then he will see how powerless death is and how completely conquered. For many who at first disbelieved and mocked, afterward believed, and so scorned death as even themselves to become martyrs for Christ's sake.

**29** Now if it is by the sign of the cross and by faith in Christ that death is trampled down, then it is clear that Christ alone is the victor who has displayed trophies and victories over death, and robbed it of its power. Death used to be strong and terrible, but now, since the sojourn of the Savior and the death and resurrection of his body, it is despised; and obviously it is by the Christ who was raised up on the cross that death has been destroyed and conquered. When the sun rises after the night and the whole world is lit up by it, nobody doubts that it is the sun which has shed its light everywhere and driven away the dark. So also, now that death has been despised and trampled down since the saving manifestation of the Savior in the body and the consummation of the cross, it is clear that he is the Savior: Revealed in the body, destroying death, and daily displaying the trophies against it in his disciples.

For when you see men, weak by nature, hastening to death, not fearing the prospect of corruption, fearless of the descent into Hades, but even with eager soul challenging it, not shrinking from torture, but rather for the sake of Christ preferring instead of this present life to rush toward death; or if you see with your own eyes men and women and children, welcoming death for the sake of devotion to Christ, who is so silly or incredulous or maimed in your mind as not to realize that Christ, to whom these all bear witness, is the one who gives the victory to each, making death completely powerless over those who keep his faith and bear the sign of the cross?

No one in his right mind doubts that a snake is dead when he sees it trampled underfoot, especially when he knows how savage it used to be; nor, if he sees boys making fun of a lion, does he doubt that it is either dead or has completely lost all its strength. These things can be seen with our own eyes, and it is the same with the conquest of death. Doubt no longer, then, when you see death mocked and scorned by those who believe in Christ, that by Christ death has been destroyed, and its corruption dissolved and brought to end.

**30** What we have said so far is no small proof that death has been destroyed and that the cross of the Lord is the monument to his victory. But the resurrection of the body to immortality, which now results from the work of Christ, the common Savior and true Life of all, is more effectively proved by facts than by words to those whose mental vision is sound.

For if death has been destroyed, as we have shown, and everyone tramples it down because of Christ, then all the more he himself trampled and destroyed it in his own body. Death having been slain by Christ, what other result could there be, than the rising of his body and its being shown forth as the trophy of his victory? How could the destruction of death have been revealed at all, if the Lord's body had not been raised? But if anyone finds proof of his resurrection is not sufficient, then let him be assured by what takes place before his eyes.

Dead men cannot take action; their power lasts only till the grave. Deeds and actions toward others belong only to the living. So look at the facts in this case; the Savior is working mightily among men, and every day he is invisibly persuading many people all over the world, both within the Greek-speaking world and beyond, to turn to his faith and be obedient to his teaching. Can anyone still doubt whether the resurrection has been accomplished by the Savior, or that he is himself the Life? Does a dead man prick the consciences of men, so that they deny the traditions of their fathers and bow down before the teaching of Christ? If he is no longer active in the world, as is proper to the dead, then how is it that he causes the living to cease from their activities – the adulterer from his adultery, the murderer from killing, the unjust from greed, while the profane and godless man becomes faithful? If he did not rise, but is still dead, how is it that he drives away and pursues and overthrows the false gods, whom unbelievers think to be alive, and the demons they worship? For where Christ and his Faith are named, idolatry is destroyed and the fraud of demons is exposed; indeed, no such spirit can endure that name, but flees at the sound of it.

This is not the work of one who is dead, but of one who is alive; and specifically the work of God. It would be absurd to say that the evil spirits whom he drives out and the idols which he destroys are alive, but that he who drives out and destroys them, he whom they themselves acknowledge to be the Son of God, is dead!

**31** Those who disbelieve in the resurrection have no support in facts, if their gods and demons do not drive away the supposedly dead Christ. Rather, it is he who convicts them of being dead. We are agreed that a dead man can do nothing: yet the Savior works mightily every day, drawing men to piety, persuading them to virtue, teaching them about immortality, leading them to thirst for heavenly things, revealing the knowledge of the Father, inspiring strength in face of death, manifesting himself to each, and displacing the godlessness of idols; while the gods and demons of the unbelievers can do none of these things, but rather fall dead at Christ's presence, all their show being futile and empty. By the sign of the cross, on the contrary, all magic ceases, all witchcraft is brought to nought, all the idols are abandoned and deserted, and all irrational desire ceases, as every one looks up from earth to heaven.

Whom, then, should we call dead? Shall we call Christ dead, who brings all this to pass? But the dead have no power to do anything. Or shall we rather call death dead: death, which in no way acts, whatever, but lies as lifeless and ineffective as the dead demons and idols? The Son of God, "living and effective,"[48] works daily and brings about the salvation of all; but death is daily proved to be stripped of all its strength, and it is the idols and the demons who are dead. So no room for doubt remains concerning the resurrection of His body.

**32** He who disbelieves this bodily rising of the Lord is ignorant of the power of the Word and Wisdom of God. For if he had fully taken to himself a body, and made it his own with proper consistency, as our argument has shown, what should the Lord do with it? What was ultimately to become of that body upon which the Word had descended? Being mortal, and offered to death on behalf of all as it was, it could not do otherwise than to die; indeed, it was for that very purpose that the Savior had prepared it for himself. But it could not remain dead, because it had become the very temple of Life. It therefore died, as mortal, came again to life because of the Life within it; and its resurrection is made known through its works.

But if his resurrection is disbelieved, because he is not seen, then it is now time for those not believing to deny the very course

---

[48] Hebrews 4:12.

of nature. For it is a property of God not to be seen, but to be known by his works, just as was said above. So if there were no works, then they would have grounds for disbelief; but when the works cry out and prove the fact so clearly, why do they choose too deny the risen life that is so manifestly shown? Even if their mental faculties are defective, surely their eyes can give them indisputable proof of the power and divinity of Christ. A blind man cannot see the sun, but he knows that it is above the earth from the warmth it gives; so let those who are still in the blindness of unbelief recognize the divinity of Christ and the resurrection he has accomplished through his manifested power in others.

It is clear he would not be expelling demons and despoiling idols if he were dead, for the spirits would not obey a dead man. But if his very name drives them out, then clearly he is not dead; but rather the demons, who see things unseen by men, would know if Christ were dead and would refuse to obey him. But the demons see what ungodly men do not believe – that he is God – and for that reason they flee and fall down before him, crying out what as they said while he was in the body, "We know who you are, the Holy One of God," [49]and, "Ah, what have I to do with you, Son of God? I implore you, do not torment me!"[50]

Since the demons confess him, and his works bear witness to him day by day, it must be evident, and let none presume to doubt it, that the Savior has raised his own body, and that he is the true Son of God, being from him as the Father's own Word and Wisdom and Power. This is he who in these last days assumed a body for the salvation of us all, and taught the world about the Father, destroyed death, and granted incorruption to all through the promise of the resurrection, having raised his own body as its first-fruits, and displayed it by the sign of the cross as the monument to his victory over death and its corruption.

---

[49] Luke 4:34.

[50] Mathew 8:28; Mark 5:7.

# Answering the Jews

## Introduction

Having completed his apologetic showing why the incarnation, cross, and resurrection were necessary in order to reverse the penalty of the fall, because death had to be overcome, now Athanasius directly confronts the Jews regarding their inability or refusal to recognize Jesus as the Christ and incarnate God. Athanasius draws upon both scripture and history to make his case.

## Refutation of the Jews

**1** We have dealt thus far with the Incarnation of our Savior, and have found clear proof of the resurrection of his body and his victory over death. Let us now go further and respond to the unbelief and the ridicule with which Jews and Gentiles respectively regard these same facts. It seems that in both cases the points at issue are the same, namely the unseemliness of the cross and of God the Word's becoming man. But we have no hesitation in taking up the argument against these objections, for the proofs on our side are extremely clear.

The unbelieving Jews may be refuted from the scriptures which they themselves read; for from beginning to end the inspired book clearly teaches these things both in its entirety and in its actual words. Prophets foretold the marvel of the Virgin and of the birth from her, saying, "Behold, the virgin shall conceive and bear a Son, and shall call his name *Immanuel,* [51] which means *God with us.*"[52] And Moses, that truly great man in whose word the Jews trust so implicitly, also recognized the importance and truth of the matter. He puts it thus: "A star shall rise out of Jacob, and a man shall rise out of Israel. He shall break in pieces the rulers of

---

[51] Isaiah 7:14.

[52] Matthew 1:23

Moab."[53] And, again, "How beautiful are your dwellings, O Jacob, your tents, O Israel. Like wooded valleys offering shade, and like gardens by the rivers, like tents the Lord pitched, like cedars beside the waters. A man shall come forth from his seed, and he shall rule many nations."[54] And, again, Isaiah says, "Before the child shall be old enough to call father or mother, one shall take the power of Damascus and the spoils of Samaria from under the eyes of the king of Assyria."[55] These words, then, foretell that a man shall appear.

And scripture proclaims further that the one who is to come is Lord of all, saying, "Behold, the Lord sits on a swift cloud and shall come to Egypt, and the man-made images of Egypt shall be shaken."[56] And it is from Egypt also that the Father calls him back, saying, "Out of Egypt have I called my Son."[57]

**2** Moreover, the Scriptures are not silent even about his death. On the contrary, they refer to it with the utmost clearness. For they have not feared to speak also of its cause – that he endured it not for his own sake, but for the immortality and salvation of all – and they record also the plotting of the Jews against him and all the indignities which he suffered at their hands. Certainly no one who reads the scriptures can plead ignorance of the facts as an excuse for error. There is this passage, for instance: "A man that is afflicted and knows how to bear weakness, for his face is turned away. He was dishonored and not esteemed. He bears our sins and suffers for our sakes, and we considered him to be distressed and afflicted and ill-treated. But he was wounded because of our lawlessness and was made weak because of our sins. Chastisement for our peace was upon him, and by his bruise we are healed."[58]

---

[53] Numbers 24:17.

[54] Numbers 24:5-7.

[55] Isaiah 8:4.

[56] Isaiah 19:1.

[57] Hosea 11:1.

[58] Isaiah 53:3-5.

Be amazed at the Word's love for human beings, that he is dishonored for our sake, that we might be honored "For we all," it goes on, "have strayed like sheep, man has strayed from his path, and the Lord has delivered him up for our sins; and he himself did not open his mouth at the ill-treatment. Like a sheep he was led to slaughter, and as a lamb is silent before its shearer, so he opened not his mouth; in his humiliation his judgment was taken away."[59] Then, so that no one may suppose from his suffering that he is a mere human being, scripture shows what power worked in him: "Who shall declare of what lineage he comes?" it says, "for his life is taken away from the earth. By the lawlessnesses of my people he was brought to death. I will appoint evil men for his burial and the rich men for his death. For he committed no lawlessness, nor was deceit found in his mouth. The Lord wishes to cleanse him of his wound."[60]

**3** You have heard the prophecy of his death. Do you now want to know what is indicated about the cross? For even this is not passed over in silence: on the contrary, the saints proclaim it with great plainness. Moses foretells it first, with a loud voice, saying, "You shall see your Life hanging before your eyes, and shall not believe."[61] After him the prophets also testified, saying, "But as an innocent lamb I was brought to be offered, though I was ignorant of it. They plotted evil against me, saying, 'Come, let us cast wood into his bread, and wipe him out from the land of the living."[62] And, again, "They pierced my hands and my feet, they counted all my bones, they divided my garments among them, and cast lots for my clothing."[63] Now a death lifted up taking place on wood can be none other than the cross; it is only in that death that the hands and feet are pierced.

---

[59] Isaiah 53:6-8.

[60] Isaiah 53:8-10.

[61] Deuteronomy 28:66.

[62] Jeremiah 11:18-19.

[63] Psalm 21:17-19.

Besides this, since the time the Savior dwelt among men, all nations everywhere have begun to know God; and this too holy scripture expressly mentions. "There shall be the Root of Jesse," it says, "and he shall arise up to rule the nations. On Him the nations shall set their hope."[64]

These are just a few things in proof of what has taken place; but indeed all scripture is full of things that refute the unbelief of the Jews. For which of the righteous and holy prophets and patriarchs named in the divine scriptures ever had his bodily birth from a virgin only? Was not Abel born from Adam, Enoch from Jared, Noah from Lamech, Abraham from Terah, Isaac from Abraham, and Jacob from Isaac? Was not Judah from Jacob, and Moses and Aaron from Amram? Was not Samuel the son of Elkanah, David the son of Jesse, Solomon the son of David, Hezekiah of Ahaz, Josiah of Amon, Isaiah of Amos, Jeremiah of Hilkiah and Ezekiel of Buzi? Did not each of these have a father as author of his being? Then who is born of a virgin only? For the prophet makes much of this sign. And of all those people, which had his birth announced to the world by a star in the heavens? When Moses was born his parents hid him. David was unknown even in his own neighborhood, so that mighty Samuel himself was ignorant of his existence and asked whether Jesse had yet another son. Abraham had already become great when he was known to his kin. But with Christ it was otherwise. The witness to his birth was not a human, but a star, shining in the heavens from which he came down.

**4** But what king ever reigned and took trophies from his enemies "before he was able to cry out 'father' or 'mother,'"[65] Was not David thirty years old when he came to the throne and Solomon a grown young man? Did not Joash begin his reign at the age of seven, and Josiah, after him, at about the same age, both of them fully able by that time to call father or mother?

---

[64] Isaiah 11:10.

[65] Isaiah 8:4.

Who is there, then, that was reigning and despoiling his enemies almost before he was born? Let the Jews, who have investigated the matter, tell us if there was ever such a king in Israel or Judah – a king upon whom all the nations set their hopes and had peace, instead of being at enmity with him on every side! As long as Jerusalem stood, there was constant war between them, and they all fought against Israel. The Assyrians oppressed Israel, the Egyptians persecuted them, the Babylonians fell upon them, and, strange to relate, even the Syrians their neighbors were at war with them. And did not David make war against Moab and smite the Syrians, and Hezekiah fear the boasting of Sennacherib? Did not Amalek make war on Moses and the Amorites oppose him, and did not the inhabitants of Jericho array themselves against Joshua the son of Nun? Did not the nations always regard Israel with implacable hostility? Then it is worth inquiring who it is, on whom the nations are to set their hopes. Obviously there must be someone, for the prophet could not have told a lie.

But did any of the holy prophets or patriarchs of old die on a cross for the salvation of all? Was any of them wounded and destroyed for the healing of all? Did the idols of Egypt fall down before any righteous man or king that came there? Abraham certainly went to Egypt, but idolatry prevailed just the same; and Moses was born there, but the deluded worship was unchanged.

**5** Again, does Scripture tell of anyone who was pierced in hands and feet or hung upon a tree at all, and by means of a cross perfected his sacrifice for the salvation of all? It was not Abraham, for he died in his bed, as did also Isaac and Jacob. Moses and Aaron died on the mountain, and David in his house, without anybody plotting against him. For though he had been sought by Saul, he was preserved unharmed. Isaiah was sawn asunder, but he was not hung on a tree. Jeremiah was shamefully treated but he did not die under condemnation. Ezekiel suffered, but he did so not on behalf of the people, but indicating what was going to happen to them. Moreover, all these, even when they suffered, were but men, like other men. But he whom the scriptures declare to suffer on behalf of all is called not merely man but the Life of all, even though in fact he shared our human nature. "You shall see your life hanging before your eyes,"[66] they say, and "Who shall declare of what lineage he comes?"[67] With all the saints we can trace their descent from the beginning, and see exactly how each came to be; but the divine scripture maintains that the lineage of him who is the Life cannot be declared.

Who is it, then, of whom divine scriptures say these things? Who is so great that even the prophets foretell such mighty things about him? No one in the scriptures at all, save the common Savior of all, the Word of God, our Lord Jesus Christ. He is the one who proceeded from a virgin, and appeared on earth as man, whose earthly lineage cannot be declared, because he alone derives his body from no human father, but from a virgin alone. We can trace the paternal descent of David and Moses and of all the patriarchs. But with the Savior we cannot do so. For it was he himself who caused the star to announce his bodily birth, and it was fitting that the Word, when he came down from heaven, should have his sign in heaven too, and fitting that the King of creation, on his coming forth, should be clearly known by all the world. He was born in Judea, yet men from Persia came to worship him.

It is he who, even before his appearing in the body, won the victory over the opposing demons and a triumph over idolatry, that is, all the heathen who from every region have turned from the tradition of their fathers and the false worship of idols and are now placing their hope in Christ and dedicating themselves to him. The thing is happening before our very eyes, here in Egypt; and thereby another prophecy is fulfilled, for at no other time have the Egyptians ceased from their false worship save when the Lord of all, riding as on a cloud, came down here in the body and brought the error of idols to nothing and won over everyone to himself, and through himself to the Father.

---

[66] Deuteronomy 28:66.

[67] Isaiah 53:8.

He is the one who was crucified with the sun and moon as witnesses; and by his death salvation has come to all men, and all creation has been redeemed. He is the Life of all, and it is he who, like a sheep, gave up his own body to death, his life for ours and our salvation.

**6** Yet the Jews disbelieve this. This argument does not satisfy them. Therefore let them be persuaded by other reasons in their own oracles. Of whom, for instance, do the prophets say "I was made manifest to those who did not seek me; I was found by those who had not asked for me. I said, 'See, here I am,' to the nation that did not call on my name. I stretched out my hands to a disobedient and rebellious people."[68]

Who is this that was made manifest, one might ask the Jews? If the prophet is speaking of himself, then they must tell us how he was first hidden, in order to be manifested afterwards. And, again, what kind of prophet is this, who was not only revealed after being hidden, but also stretched out his hands upon the cross? Those things happened to none of those righteous men: they happened only to the Word of God who, being bodiless by nature, appeared in a body for our sake and suffered for us all.

And if even this is not enough for them, there is other overwhelming evidence by which they may be silenced. The scripture says, "Strengthen the weak hands feeble knees; take courage, you of little faith, be strong and do not fear. Behold, our God will recompense judgment, he himself will come and save us. Then the eyes of the blind shall be opened and the ears of the deaf shall hear, and the mute tongue shall speak clearly."[69] What can they say to this, or how can they look it in the face at all? For the prophecy does not only declare that God will dwell here, it also makes known the signs and the time of his coming. When God comes, it says, the blind will see, the lame will walk, the deaf will hear and the stammerers will speak distinctly. Can the Jews tell us

[68] Isaiah 65:1-2.

[69] Isaiah 35:3-6.

when such signs occurred in Israel, or when anything of the kind took place at all in Judea? The leper Naaman was cleansed, it is true, but no deaf man heard nor did any lame man walk. Elijah and Elisha raised the dead, but no one blind from birth received his sight.

Raising the dead is truly a great thing, but it is not like the wonder wrought by the Savior. And surely, since the Scriptures have not kept silence about the leper and the dead son of the widow, if a lame man had walked and a blind man had received his sight, they would have mentioned these as well. Their silence on these points proves that the events had never taken place before.

So when did these things happen, apart from when the Word of God himself came in the body? Was it not when he came that lame men walked and stammerers spoke clearly and men blind from birth were given sight? And even the Jews who saw it testified to the fact that such things had never before occurred. "Since the world began, it has never been heard of that anyone should open the eyes of a man born blind. If this man were not from God, he could do nothing."[70]

7 But surely they cannot fight against plain facts. So it may be that, without denying what is written, they will maintain that they are still waiting for these things to happen, and that the Word of God is yet to come, for that is a topic about which they are always chattering most brazenly, in spite of all the evidence against them. But on this one point, above all, they shall be refuted all the more, not by ourselves but by the most wise Daniel, for he signifies the actual date of the Savior's coming as well as his Divine sojourn in our midst, saying, "Seventy weeks are determined for your people and for your holy city, to make an end of sin, and for sins to be sealed up and iniquities blotted out, and to make reconciliation for wrongdoings, to seal up vision and prophecy, and to anoint the Holy One of holies. You shall know therefore and understand

[70] John 9:32-33.

from the going forth of the word to restore and build Jerusalem, until Christ the Prince."[71]

Perhaps regarding the other prophecies, they could find excuses to put off what is written to a future time, but what can they say to this? How can they face it at all? Not only does it expressly refer to the Anointed One, that is the Christ, it declares that he who is to be anointed is not merely human but is himself the holy of holies! And it says that Jerusalem is to stand until his coming, and then prophet and vision shall cease in Israel.

David was anointed of old, and Solomon, and Hezekiah, but Jerusalem and the place still stood, and prophets were prophesying – Gad and Asaph and Nathan, and later Isaiah and Hosea and Amos and the others. Moreover, those men who were anointed were called holy, but none of them was called the holy of holies.

Nor is it any use for the Jews to take refuge in the Babylonian captivity, and say that Jerusalem did not exist then, for what about the prophets? It is a fact that when the people went into exile, Daniel and Jeremiah were there, and Ezekiel and Haggai and Zechariah also prophesied.

**8** So the Jews are indulging in fiction, and transferring they present time into the future. For when did prophet and vision cease from Israel, if not now, when Christ, the holy of holies, has come? In fact it is a sign and a great proof of the coming of the Word that Jerusalem no longer stands, neither is any prophet raised up nor vision revealed among them. And it is natural that it should be so – for when he who was indicated had come, what need is there any longer of any sign to indicate him? And now that the reality has come, what further need is there of the shadow?

For this was the reason for their prophesying at all, that is, until the true righteousness should come, who redeems for the sins of all. For the same reason Jerusalem stood until the same time,

---

[71] Daniel 9:24-25.

in order that there men might be prepared by the types before the truth was known. So, of course, once the holy of holies had come, both vision and prophecy were sealed, and the kingdom of Jerusalem ceased at the same time. Kings were to be anointed among them only until the holy of holies was anointed.

Moses also prophesied that the kingdom of the Jews would stand until that One should come, saying, "A ruler shall not fail from Judah nor a prince from his loins, until the things laid up for him shall come and the expectation of the nations himself."[72] So the Savior himself proclaimed, "For all the Prophets and the Law prophesied until John."[73] So if there were still king or prophet or vision among the Jews, they would do well to deny that Christ is come; but if there is neither king nor vision, and since that time all prophecy has been sealed up and the city and temple are taken, then how can they be so perverse as to see what has happened and yet to deny Christ? And when they see the nations forsaking idols and setting their hopes through Christ on the God of Israel, why do they deny Christ who was born of the root of Jesse according to the flesh, and reigns henceforth? If the nations were worshiping some other god, and not confessing the God of Abraham and Isaac and Jacob and Moses, then they would do well to argue that God had not come. But if the heathen are honoring the same God who gave the law to Moses and the promises to Abraham – the God whose word the Jews dishonored – then why do they not recognize, or rather why do they deliberately refuse to see, that the Lord prophesied in the scriptures has shone forth in the world and appeared to it in a body?

Scripture declares it repeatedly. "God is the Lord and has revealed himself to us,"[74] and again, "He sent forth his Word and healed them."[75] And again, "It was no ambassador, nor an angel

---

[72] Genesis 49:10.

[73] Matthew 11:13.

[74] Psalm 117:27.

[75] Psalm 106:20.

who saved us, but the Lord himself."[76] The Jews are suffering like one out of his mind who sees the earth lit up by the sun, but denies the sun that lights it up. For when the one they expect comes, what more will he do? Call the heathen? But they are called already. Cause prophet and king and vision to cease? This too has already happened. To expose the godlessness of idolatry? It is already exposed and condemned. Or to destroy death? It is already destroyed.

What then has not come to pass that the Christ must do? What is there left out or unfulfilled that the Jews should disbelieve so light-heartedly? For, as we see, there is no longer any king or prophet nor Jerusalem nor sacrifice nor vision among them, yet the whole earth is filled with the knowledge of God, and the nations, forsaking godlessness, are now taking refuge with the God of Abraham through the Word, our Lord Jesus Christ.

Surely, then, it must be plain even to the most shameless that the Christ has come, and that he has enlightened all men everywhere, and given them the true and divine teaching about his Father. In this way one can rightly answer the Jews from these and many more passages from the divine scriptures.

---

[76] Isaiah 63:9.

# Bibliography


Athanasius. "On the Incarnation of the Word." Translated by Alexander Walker. In *The Nicene and Post Nicene Fathers,* edited by Philip Schaff and Henry Wace, Second Series, Volume 4, Hendrickson, 1994.

Athanasius. *On the Incarnation: Greek Original and English Translation.* Translated by John Behr. St Vladimir's Seminary Press, 2011.

Athanasius. *On the Incarnation: The Treatise De Incarnatione Verbi Dei.* Translated by a religious of SPCK. Crestwood, NY: St. Vladimir's Seminary Press, 1996.

Athanasius. *St. Athanasius on the Incarnation.* Translated by Archibald Robertson. 3rd ed. David Nutt, 1911.

Eusebius. *Eusebius: The Church History; a New Translation with Commentary.* Translated by Paul Maier. Kregel Publications, 1999.

Melito. *On Pascha.* Translated by Alistair Stewart. 2nd ed. St Vladimirs Seminary Press, 2020.

"On the Passover – Melito of Sardis." Kerux: A Journal of Biblical Theology 4:1 (May 1989). Accessed April 1, 2024. https://kerux.com/doc/0401A1.asp.

Holmes, Michael W., editor. *The Apostolic Fathers: Greek Texts and English Translations.* 3rd ed. Baker Academic, 2007.

Richardson, Cyril C. *Early Christian Fathers.* 1st Touchstone ed., Simon & Schuster, 1996.

# Scripture Index

## Old Testament

**Genesis**

1:1....144
1:26....22, 156
1:28....22
2:16–18....145
2:17....128
2:23....7
4:3–8....6
4:7....5
12:1–3....9
13:14–16....9
15:5....9, 21
18:27....14
37:9....63
49:10....186

**Exodus**

2:14....6
3:11....14
12:8....136
12:11–30....121
20:13–17....44
32:7....33
32:9....33
32:31....33

**Leviticus**

19:18....42

**Numbers**

6:25....38
12:7....14, 27
16:33....32
18:27....20
24:5–7....178
24:17....178
27:16....37

**Deuteronomy**

1:16....45
4:2....45
4:34....20
9:12....33
9:13....33
12:25....38

14:2....................................39
18:3–5....................................51
19:10....................................133
21:23....................................169
28:66....................131, 179, 182
31:7....................................110
32:8....................................20
32:15....................................5
32:39....................................37

**Joshua**

1:1....................................14
1:6....................................110
1:21....................................98
4:16–18....................................26
5:11....................................37
5:17–26....................................35
11:2....................................21
14:4....................................14
19:26....................................19
38:11....................................16

**1 Samuel**

2:6....................................37
2:7....................................37
2:10....................................11

**1 Kings**

8:60....................................37
9:4....................................38

**2 Kings**

5:7....................................37
19:19....................................37

**2 Chronicles**

31:14....................................20

**Nehemiah**

1:9....................................48

**Job**

1:1....................................14
1:21....................................98
4:16–18....................................26
5:11....................................37
5:17–26....................................35
11:2....................................21
14:4....................................14
19:26....................................19
38:11....................................16

**Psalms**

1:3....................................68
2:1–2....................................131
2:7....................................24
2:11....................................97, 100
3:5....................................19
4:2....................................46
4:5....................................104
11:4–6....................................12
15:10....................................166
17:26....................................29
18:1–3....................................19
21:7–9....................................13
21:17–19....................................179

23:1 .......... 33
23:7 .......... 169
26:15 .......... 110
27:7 .......... 19
30:19 .......... 12
31:1 .......... 32
32:9 .......... 62
33:12–18 .......... 17
34:4 .......... 133
34:14 .......... 133
36:11 .......... 44
36:35–37 .......... 12
37:9 .......... 11
39:2 .......... 38
48:15 .......... 32
49:14 .......... 32
49:16–23 .......... 24
50:1–19 .......... 15
58:6 .......... 113
66:1 .......... 38
68:31–32 .......... 32
78:13 .......... 37
78:36 .......... 12
79:9–10 .......... 48
81:6–7 .......... 147
88:21 .......... 14
103:4 .......... 24
106:20 .......... 186
110:1 .......... 24
117:18 .......... 34
117:19 .......... 30
117:26 .......... 50
117:27 .......... 186
138:7 .......... 20
141:5 .......... 35
144:18 .......... 38
150:6 .......... 97

**Proverbs**

1:23–33 .......... 36
2:21 .......... 11
3:4 .......... 100
3:12 .......... 34
3:28 .......... 102
3:34 .......... 20, 59
7:3 .......... 5
10:12 .......... 31
18:17 .......... 68
20:27 .......... 16
21:6 .......... 44
24:12 .......... 22
31:9 .......... 45

**Isaiah**

1:16–20 .......... 8
1:23 .......... 46
3:5 .......... 5
3:10 .......... 133
5:26 .......... 86
6:3 .......... 23

7:14 ... 177
8:4 ... 178, 180
11:1 ... 48
11:10 ... 180
13:11 ... 37
19:1 ... 178
26:20 ... 31
29:13 ... 12
35:3–6 ... 183
40:10 ... 22
50:8 ... 138
52:5 ... 72, 103
53:1–12 ... 13
53:3–5 ... 178
53:6–8 ... 179
53:7 ... 131
53:8 ... 182
53:8–10 ... 179
53:9 ... 161
57:16 ... 97
58:6 ... 82
60:17 ... 27
63:9 ... 187
64:4 ... 23, 107
65:1–2 ... 183
66:2 ... 11, 44
66:18 ... 68

**Jeremiah**

5:4 ... 103
9:23 ... 11
11:18–19 ... 179
11:19 ... 131

**Ezekiel**

3:18 ... 97
33:11–27 ... 8
36:23 ... 37
37:12 ... 31
48:12 ... 20

**Daniel**

7:10 ... 23
9:24–25 ... 185

**Hosea**

11:1 ... 178

**Habakkuk**

2:14 ... 159

**Zechariah**

14:5 ... 52

**Malachi**

1:11 ... 51
3:1 ... 18

**New Testament**

**Matthew**

1:23 ... 177
2:2 ... 63
3:12 ... 107
3:15 ... 85
5:3 ... 98

5:5....44
5:7....11
5:26....43
5:39....43
5:40....43
5:44....43, 104
6:5....47
6:9–13....47
6:10....109
6:12....100
6:13....101
6:16....47
7:1....98
7:6....48
7:12....42
8:17....91
10:10....51
10:16....91
10:22....52
10:36....109
10:40....49
11:13....186
12:31....50
12:33....61
12:33–37....50
13:3....18
15:13....72, 80
15:19....46
19:4–6....144
19:12....87
19:18....44
20:22....113
21:9....49-50
22:37–39....42
22:38....50
23:27....82
24:4....46
24:10....52
24:24....52
24:30....52
24:31....49, 52
24:42....52
26:24....30
26:41....101
26:55....109
27:52....67
28:19....46

**Mark**

5:7....176
7:6....12
7:21....46
9:35....99
9:43....107
10:38....113
14:38....101
14:61....110

**Luke**

1:53....37

4:34 ..... 176
6:20 ..... 98
6:27 ..... 43, 104
6:29 ..... 43
6:30 ..... 43
6:31 ..... 11
6:36–38 ..... 98
10:18 ..... 169
11:50 ..... 97
12:35 ..... 52
17:1 ..... 30
19:10 ..... 157, 159
24:39 ..... 86

**John**

1:3 ..... 144
3:5 ..... 157
3:8 ..... 82, 101
4:2 ..... 101
4:10 ..... 78
4:11 ..... 97
4:16 ..... 96
5:19 ..... 66
5:29 ..... 113
5:43 ..... 50
6:33 ..... 58, 78
7 ..... 101
7:1 ..... 108
8 ..... 102
9:32–33 ..... 184
10:7 ..... 80, 83
10:37–38 ..... 161
12:27 ..... 113
12:28 ..... 110
12:32 ..... 169
12:33 ..... 169
18:37 ..... 106
19:9 ..... 110
19:31 ..... 109

**Acts**

1:25 ..... 66
2:24 ..... 97, 171
2:31 ..... 166
4:27 ..... 36, 48
7:52 ..... 100
8:21 ..... 104
9:7 ..... 110
10:41 ..... 86
10:42 ..... 97
12:4 ..... 120
13:22 ..... 14
13:51 ..... 108
14:23 ..... 54
15:3 ..... 97
15:7 ..... 97
16:12 ..... 98
16:20 ..... 112
17:28 ..... 142
19:31 ..... 112

20:35....................................4
21:11....................................50
21:14....................................109
22:20....................................6
26:18....................................36
26:26....................................167

**Romans**

1....................................vii
1:3....................................63, 78, 85
1:25....................................154
1:26–27....................................148
1:29–31....................................46
1:29–32....................................23
4:7–9....................................32
6:4....................................63
8:5....................................59
8:11....................................97
12:9....................................46
12:10....................................102
13:1....................................111
14:10....................................100

**1 Corinthians**

1:7....................................85
1:20....................................62
1:21....................................158
1:31....................................11
2:9....................................23, 107
2:10....................................82
3:1....................................71
3:16....................................62
4:4....................................77
4:8....................................99
6:2....................................103
6:9....................................62, 81, 100
6:14....................................97
7:22....................................76
7:36....................................50
9:15....................................77
9:27....................................73
11:23....................................7
12:21....................................25
14:25....................................99
15:8....................................78
15:23....................................24
15:28....................................97
15:53–55....................................165
15:55....................................171
15:58....................................102
16:22....................................49

**2 Corinthians**

1:22....................................101
3:2....................................103
4:14....................................97
5:10....................................100
5:14–15....................................152
5:15....................................102
6:7....................................98
8:21....................................100

10:1....102
10:17....11

**Galatians**

1:1....104
2:2....102
2:9....6
3:13....52, 168
5:17....100
5:19–21....46
6:7....99
6:9....22
6:12....82

**Ephesians**

1:13....98
1:14....101
1:18....37
2:2....169
2:5....97
2:14....169
2:16....86
3:17–19....159
4:2....91
4:26....104
5:5....103
5:25....93
6:11–17....93
6:14....97
6:18....104

**Philippians**

1:1....97
1:27....99
2:4....107
2:16....102-103
3:20....3
3:21....97
4:10....96
4:13....87
4:15....103
7:1....117
12:3....108

**Colossians**

1:4....98
1:6....97
1:10....99
1:15....157
1:16....71
1:23....60, 102, 104
1:27....101
2:10....104
2:12....104
3:5....103

**1 Thessalonians**

1:4....98
2:4....75
3:13....52
5:....99
5:10....102

5:11....104
5:17....60
5:22....103

**2 Thessalonians**

1:4....103
2:15....7
3:15....103

**1 Timothy**

1:1....101
1:3....92
1:4....67
1:5....61
1:6....97
1:16....104
1:17....38
2:1....104
2:7....38
3:5....103
3:8–13....99
4:4....54
4:15....104
5:5....99
5:9....90
5:19....100
6:2....92
6:7....98
6:10....98
6:15....153

**2 Timothy**

1:16....89
2:2....28, 54
2:4....93
2:12....99
2:25....103
4:10....102

**Titus**

1:3....153
1:5....54
3:1....4

**Philemon**

3:15....89
3:18....104

**Hebrews**

1:3....24
1:5....24
1:7....24
1:13....24
2:9....152
2:14–15....164
3:2....14
3:5....27
4:12....175
5:13....102
6:18....19
10:20....169
11:3....144
11:9....3

11:35....164
11:37....14
12:1....6
12:6....34
12:28....100
13:7....45

**James**

1:4....104
4:6....20

**1 Peter**

1:1....106
1:8....97
1:13....97
1:21....97, 104
2:11....3, 43, 100
2:12....103
2:13....111
2:17....102
2:21....102
2:22....161
2:24....101
2:25....115
3:8....102
3:9....98
3:18....114
4:7....101
4:8....31
4:11....33
4:15....102
5:5....20, 102

**1 John**

3:8....101
4:2....101
4:11....97
4:16....96

**2 John**

7....101

**3 John**

8....102

**Jude**

2....96, 106
24....115

**Revelation**

1:5....106
2:9....112
3:9....55, 81
4:8....113
4:11....48
22:12....22

www.ingramcontent.com/pod-product-compliance
Lightning Source LLC
LaVergne TN
LVHW010614100826
845148LV00014B/2966

* 9 7 9 8 8 9 7 7 8 8 6 8 2 *